My Child Is Sick!

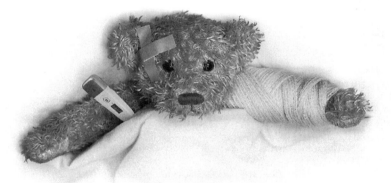

Expert Advice for Managing Common Illnesses and Injuries

Barton D. Schmitt, MD, FAAP

American Academy of Pediatrics

DEDICATED TO THE HEALTH OF ALL CHILDREN™

American Academy of Pediatrics Department of Marketing and Publications Staff

Director, Department of Marketing and Publications
   Maureen DeRosa, MPA
Director, Division of Product Development
   Mark Grimes
Manager, Consumer Publishing
   Carolyn Kolbaba
Coordinator, Product Development
   Holly Kaminski
Director, Division of Publishing and Production Services
   Sandi King, MS

Editorial Specialist
   Jason Crase
Print Production Specialist
   Shannan Martin
Manager, Art Direction and Production
   Linda Diamond
Director, Division of Marketing and Sales
   Kevin Tuley
Manager, Consumer Marketing and Sales
   Kathleen Juhl

Published by the American Academy of Pediatrics
141 Northwest Point Blvd, Elk Grove Village, IL 60007-1019
847/434-4000
Fax: 847/434-8000
www.aap.org

Cover design by Daniel Rembert
Book design by Linda Diamond
Illustrations by David Roberts

My Child Is Sick! Expert Advice for Managing Common Illnesses and Injuries was created by Barton D. Schmitt, MD, FAAP.

Library of Congress Control Number: 2010915326
ISBN: 978-1-58110-552-0

The recommendations in this publication do not indicate an exclusive course of treatment or serve as a standard of medical care. Variations, taking into account individual circumstances, may be appropriate.

Statements and opinions expressed are those of the author and not necessarily those of the American Academy of Pediatrics.

Products are mentioned for informational purposes only. Inclusion in this publication does not imply endorsement by the American Academy of Pediatrics.

Every effort is made to keep *My Child Is Sick!* consistent with the most recent advice and information possible.

Author's Disclaimer: This information is not intended to be a substitute for professional medical advice. It is provided for educational purposes only. You assume full responsibility for how you choose to use this information.

Your child's doctor has the final word. If your child's doctor tells you something that is different than what's in this book, follow your doctor's advice. Your doctor has the advantage of knowing you and your child, and taking an actual history and performing a physical examination before making a decision.

You know your child better than anyone else. If you remain uncomfortable with your child's symptoms or condition after reading this book, please call your doctor or nurse for additional assistance. Finally, if you think your child has a life-threatening condition (eg, struggling to breathe), always call 911 NOW.

CB0066
9-285   1 2 3 4 5 6 7 8 9 10

Contents

Reviewers

The author is grateful to the following individuals for their time and expertise in reviewing the triage content that has been incorporated into these guidelines:

Pediatric Call Centers: Medical Directors
- Peter Dehnel, MD, Children's Physician Network, Minneapolis, MN
- Andrew Hertz, MD, Rainbow Babies Children's Hospital, Cleveland, OH
- Randy Sterkel, MD, St. Louis Children's Hospital, St. Louis, MO
- Debra Weiner, MD, Sirona Health, Portland, ME
- Medical Advisory Board, Sykes, Toronto, Ontario, Canada
- Elaine Donoghue, MD, St. Peter's Medical Center Call Center, New Brunswick, NJ (former)
- Hanna Sherman, MD, Boston Children's Hospital Call Center, Boston, MA (former)

Physician Advisory Board: The Children's Hospital, Aurora, CO
- Francesco Beuf, MD, Boulder Pediatric Center, Boulder, CO
- Vincent DiMaria, MD, Arapahoe Park Pediatrics, Littleton, CO
- Matt Dorighi, MD, Cherry Creek Pediatrics, Denver, CO
- Max Elliott, MD, Fort Collins Youth Clinic, Fort Collins, CO
- Daniel Feiten, MD, Greenwood Pediatrics, Centennial, CO
- Nancy Greer, MD, Broomfield Pediatrics, Broomfield, CO
- Michael Kurtz, MD, Advanced Pediatric Associates, Aurora, CO
- Jay Markson, MD, Children's Medical Center, Denver, CO
- Robert Mauro, MD, Greenwood Pediatrics, Littleton, CO
- Martha Middlemist, MD, Pediatrics at 5280, Englewood, CO
- Stefan Mokrohisky, MD, Kaiser Permanente, Denver, CO
- Michelle Stanford, MD, Centennial Pediatrics, Centennial, CO

Physician Advisory Board: St. Louis Children's Hospital, St. Louis, MO

- Jay Epstein, MD, Community Pediatrician, Forest Park Pediatrics
- David Jaffe, MD, Washington University School of Medicine, Emergency Medicine
- James Keating, MD, Washington University School of Medicine, Gastroenterology/Diagnostic Center
- Katherine Kreusser, MD, Community Pediatrician, Children's Clinic
- Steve Lillpop, MD, Community Pediatrician, Jacksonville Pediatrics
- Jerome O'Neil, MD, Community Pediatrician, Southwest Pediatrics
- Rachel Orscheln, MD, Washington University School of Medicine, Infectious Disease
- Isabel Rosenbloom, MD, Community Pediatrician, Tots Thru Teens Pediatrics
- Harold Sitrin, MD, Community Pediatrician, Suburban Pediatrics
- Randy Sterkel, MD, Answer Line Medical Director, Community Pediatrician, Esse Health Pediatrics
- Mary Tillman, MD, Community Pediatrician, Tillman Pediatrics

Telephone Triage Nurses: The Children's Hospital, Aurora, CO

- Teresa Baird, RN
- Teresa Hegarty, RN
- Kris Light, RN
- Kathleen Martinez, RN
- Kelli Massaro, RN
- Ann Petersen-Smith, RN, PNP
- Liz Stober, RN

Telephone Triage Nurses: Other Sites

- Nancy Berryman, RN, Minneapolis, MN
- Barbara Byrne, RN, Tigard, OR
- Katrina Davis, RN, PNP, Salem, OR
- Jenny DuFresne, RN, Phoenix, AZ
- Alane Hall, RN, Denver, CO
- Suzanne Haydt, RN, Tucson, AZ
- Nicole Leujten, RN, Denver, CO

- Melissa Masson, RN, London, Ontario, Canada
- Cheryl Patterson, RN, Evergreen, WA
- Teresa Pounds, RN, Maryville, TN
- Lisa Swerczek, RN, St. Louis, MO
- Michelle Violette, RN, London, Ontario, Canada
- Suzanne Wells, RN, St. Louis, MO

Pediatric Emergency Medicine Specialists
- Joan Bothner, MD, Aurora, CO
- Peter O'Hanley, MD, Moncton, New Brunswick, Canada
- David Thompson, MD, Berwyn, IL (adult emergency medicine)

Pediatric Subspecialists: The Children's Hospital, Aurora, CO (Unless Otherwise Noted)
- Adolescent Medicine: David Kaplan, MD; Trina Anglin, MD; Eric Sigel, MD
- Allergy: James Shira, MD; Dan Atkins, MD
- Breastfeeding: Maya Bunik, MD; Lisbeth Gabrielski, RN; Marianne Neifert, MD
- Cardiology: Michael Schaffer, MD; James Wiggins, MD; Robert Wolfe, MD; Henry Sondheimer, MD
- Dentistry: William Mueller, DDS; Elizabeth Shick, DDS
- Dermatology: William Weston, MD; Joseph Morelli, MD
- Diabetes: Georgeanna Klingensmith, MD
- Ear, Nose, and Throat: Kenneth Chan, MD
- Endocrinology: Michael Kappy, MD
- Gastroenterology: Ronald Sokol, MD; Judy Sondheimer, MD; Sara Fidanza, RN, PNP
- General Pediatrics: Steven Poole, MD; Stephen Berman, MD; Robert Brayden, MD; Allison Kempe, MD; Maya Bunik, MD
- Hematology: Taru Hays, MD
- Infectious Diseases: James K. Todd, MD; Mary Glode, MD; Mark Abzug, MD; Brian Lauer, MD; Elizabeth McFarland, MD; Ann-Christine Nyquist, MD; Harley Rotbart, MD; John Ogle, MD
- Neonatology: Susan Niermeyer, MD; Elizabeth Thilo, MD; Adam Rosenberg, MD

- Neurology: Paul Moe, MD; Paul Levisohn, MD
- Nutrition: Nancy Krebs, MD
- Ophthalmology: Robert King, MD
- Orthopedics: Robert Eilert, MD; Frank Chang, MD
- Pulmonary Medicine: Frank Accurso, MD; Jeffrey Wagener, MD; Gwendolyn Kerby, MD; Scott Sagel, MD; Monica Federico, MD
- Rheumatology: Roger Hollister, MD
- Sports Medicine: Brooke Pengel, MD
- Toxicology: Richard Dart, MD, Medical Director, Rocky Mountain Poison and Drug Center; William D. King, RPh, MPH, DrPH, University of Alabama School of Medicine; Erica Liebolt, MD, FACMT, University of Alabama School of Medicine
- Urology: Martin Koyle, MD

American Academy of Pediatrics Appointed Reviewers

- Jack Swanson, MD, FAAP, Former Chair, AAP Committee on Practice and Ambulatory Medicine
- Allan Lieberthal, MD, FAAP, Former Member, AAP Committee on Practice and Ambulatory Medicine
- Jennifer Shu, MD, FAAP, Medical Editor, HealthyChildren.org, official AAP Web site for parents

Practicing Pediatricians

- Justin Alvey, MD, Layton, UT
- John Benbow, MD, Concord, NC
- Barbara Brundage, MD, Derry, NH
- Thomas Foels, MD, Williamsville, NY
- Fred Hamburg, MD, Springfield, MO
- George Miller, MD, Salem, OR
- Cajsa Schumacher, MD, Albany, NY
- Kiki Traylor MD, Denver, CO
- Paul Tschetter, MD, Denver, CO
- Sarah Van Scoy, MD, Denver, CO
- Joseph Vander-Walde, MD, Kaiser Permanente Mid-Atlantic
- Wallace White, MD, Denver, CO

Introduction

Most of the time your child is well—hungry at mealtime, sleeps soundly. Your family has fun together. The days fly by.

Then without warning, your child is sick or injured. You're uncertain what to do next. Should you call your child's doctor? Should you go to the emergency department? Can you treat your child at home? What's the current best advice for relieving your child's symptom?

That's why you have this book.

The first purpose of *My Child Is Sick!* is to help you determine how sick your child is and if you need to call your child's doctor. The second purpose is to help you treat your child at home when it is safe to do so.

Here's what the book covers.

- The most common illnesses and injuries of childhood. At some point your child will develop most of these symptoms. You won't have to search through endless descriptions of uncommon conditions to find what you need.
- Decision charts on when to call your child's doctor and when it's safe to treat your child at home. It teaches what symptoms are normal during the course of an illness or recovery from an injury. It also describes which symptoms are cause for concern and gives a specific time frame in which you need to call your child's doctor. About half the time, you can safely take care of your child at home without even calling your doctor.
- Specific, in-depth home care (treatment) advice for each symptom. You won't have to guess about the details of how to make your child feel better. And the advice is identical to that given by telephone nurses in most pediatric offices and hospital-based advice lines.
- Drug dosage tables for the most commonly used nonprescription medicines.
- Specific reassurance to help you manage nonserious symptoms.

Finally, you are an important member of your child's health care team. Trust your parental instincts; they are a special safeguard for protecting your child. And never underestimate your common sense and potential to learn more about common illnesses and injuries. This book can empower you to provide optimal care for your sick child.

Using This Book

Select a Chapter

Choose the chapter that most closely matches your child's symptoms.

- If your child has more than one symptom, address the most serious symptom first. The most serious symptom is the symptom that potentially could cause the most harm to your child. (For example, for nosebleed and head injury together, use Chapter 2, Head Injury.) If you aren't sure which chapter to use, use more than one.
- Don't use Chapter 49, Fever, unless fever is your child's only symptom. If your child also has a cough, diarrhea, or another symptom, go to that chapter instead of fever.
- Choosing the appropriate symptom is very important because it leads you to the best information for your child's illness or injury.

Read the Chapter

Each chapter has 3 parts: Definition, When to Call Your Doctor, and Home Care Advice

1. **Definition.** Go to the selected chapter and read the definition to be sure it's a good fit for your child's problem. If not, consider related symptoms listed under the section, "See More Appropriate Topic (Instead of This One)."

2. **When to Call Your Doctor.** Following the "Definition" section in each chapter, there is a decision chart that gives options for what action you should take, including Call 911 Now, Call Your Doctor Now, Call Your Doctor Within 24 Hours, Call Your Doctor During Weekday Office Hours, and Parent Care at Home. Below each response is a list of symptoms or reasons for using that option. Read through these bulleted items. Read from top to bottom and don't skip any symptoms or reasons. The purpose of these is to help you determine the seriousness of your child's illness or injury. If your child has even one of the emergent symptoms (Call 911 Now) or other

Call Your Doctor Now symptoms, stop reading the list of symptoms and take the action suggested in the heading at the top of the list. If the recommendation is to call your doctor within 24 hours or during weekday office hours, refer to the Home Care Advice section to help you keep your child comfortable until then.

When to Call Your Doctor: Parent Responses

One of the purposes of this book is to help you determine how sick your child is. Then it is time to make a decision and act. By reading the "When to Call Your Doctor" questions and using your common sense, you should be able to fit your child into 1 of the following 5 "When to Call Your Doctor" categories:

Call 911 Now (Your Child May Need an Ambulance)

- **Definition:** Your child may have a life-threatening emergency.
- **Action:** Immediately call 911 or your emergency medical response system.

Call Your Doctor Now (Night or Day)

- **Definition:** Your child may have a non–life-threatening emergency or urgent condition.
- **Action:** Call your child's doctor immediately. If you can't reach your doctor within 60 minutes, go to the nearest emergency department (ED) by car. If you don't have a doctor, go to the nearest ED now.

Call Your Doctor Within 24 Hours (Between 9:00 am and 4:00 pm)

- **Definition:** Your child probably has a nonurgent illness that may require a specific test (eg, throat culture) or an antibiotic (eg, for an ear infection). Your child may need to be seen, but it can safely wait for up to 24 hours.
- **Action:** If the office is open, call now. If the office is closed now but will be open within 24 hours, call when it opens. If the office won't be open within the next 24 hours, call your doctor's answering service between 9:00 am and 4:00 pm on any day of the week (including weekends and holidays) for assistance. If you don't have a doctor, go to an urgent care center or ED within the next 24 hours.

Call Your Doctor During Weekday Office Hours

- **Definition:** Your child has a nonurgent symptom or illness that has lasted longer than expected (eg, persistent cough, localized rash) but usually carries no risk of complications. Your child may need to be seen in the office but can safely wait a few days if it's the weekend or a holiday.
- **Action:** If the office is open, call now. Otherwise, call during scheduled weekday office hours on Monday through Friday. (This category therefore excludes weekends and holidays.) If you don't have a doctor, choose a doctor and make an appointment to be seen within the next 3 days.

Parent Care at Home

- **Definition:** Your child probably has a mild illness that's usually self-limited or harmless.
- **Action:** Your child can be safely cared for by you at home. Follow the detailed home care advice provided in each topic. You don't need to call your doctor unless your child's condition becomes worse or you are uncomfortable with how your child looks or acts.

3. **Home Care Advice.** If your child has none of the Call Your Doctor symptoms, follow the home care advice listed in the final section. But watch your child carefully for any worsening or new symptoms. If your child's condition changes for the worse or you are uncomfortable with how your child looks or acts, call your child's doctor again.

Part 1

Head or Brain
Symptoms

Chapter 1

Crying

Definition

- Excessive crying, irritability, or fussiness in a child 3 months or older.
- Child is too young to tell us or show us the cause for his crying.
- Crying is the only symptom.
- If your child is crying from an illness or physical symptom, use that chapter instead of this one.

Causes
- Not caused by hunger—by this age, you should be able to recognize hunger.
- **Main Cause:** Coming down with an illness.
- **Other Common Causes:** Overtired, stressed, whining, tantrums, and separation anxiety. This chapter detects many infants with sleep problems.
- Always consider pain as a possible cause of persistent fussiness or crying. Inconsolable crying may be the only symptom initially in a young child with an ear infection or even appendicitis.
- Painful causes include earache, blocked nose from a cold, sore throat, mouth ulcers, raw diaper rash, meatal ulcer on tip of penis, and constipation.
- Teething generally doesn't cause pain or crying.

See More Appropriate Topic (Instead of This One) If
- Fever (see Chapter 49) or any symptom of illness (eg, diarrhea, constipation) (see that chapter)
- Crying from an injury (see specific injury chapter)

When to Call Your Doctor

Call 911 Now (Your Child May Need an Ambulance) If
- Not moving or very weak

Call Your Doctor Now (Night or Day) If
- Your child looks or acts very sick
- Stiff neck or bulging soft spot
- Possible injury (especially head or bone injury)
- Very irritable, screaming child for longer than 1 hour
- You are afraid you or someone might hurt or shake your baby
- Your child cannot be comforted after trying this advice for 2 hours
- Crying interferes with sleeping for longer than 2 hours

Call Your Doctor Within 24 Hours (Between 9:00 am and 4:00 pm) If
- You think your child needs to be seen
- Pain (eg, earache) suspected as cause of crying

Call Your Doctor During Weekday Office Hours If
- You have other questions or concerns
- Mild, off-and-on fussiness (acts normal when not crying) continues more than 2 days
- Excessive crying is a chronic problem

Parent Care at Home If
- Mild fussiness present fewer than 2 days and you don't think your child needs to be seen

Home Care Advice for Mild Consolable Crying

1. **Reassurance:** Most infants and toddlers become somewhat irritable and fussy when sick or overtired. Crying tells us your child is not feeling well. If the crying responds to comforting, it's probably not serious.

2. **Comforting:** Try to comfort your child by holding, rocking, or massaging her.

3. **Sleep:** If your child is tired, put him to bed. If he needs to be held, hold him quietly in a horizontal position or lie next to him. Some overtired infants need to cry themselves to sleep.

4. **Undress Your Child:** Sometimes part of her clothing is too tight or uncomfortable. Also check her skin for redness or swelling (eg, insect bite).

5. **Discontinue Medicines**
   - If your child is taking a cough or cold medicine, stop it.
   - The crying should stop within 4 hours.
   - Antihistamines (eg, Benadryl) can cause screaming and irritability in some children.
   - Pseudoephedrine (decongestant) can cause jitteriness and crying.

6. **Expected Course:** Most fussiness with illnesses resolves when the illness does. Most fussiness caused by stress or change (eg, new child care) lasts less than 1 week.

7. **Call Your Doctor If**
   - Constant crying lasts longer than 2 hours.
   - Intermittent crying lasts more than 2 days.
   - Your child becomes worse.

> **And remember, contact your doctor if your child develops any of the "Call Your Doctor" symptoms.**

Chapter 2

Head Injury

Definition

- Injuries to the head

Types of Head Injuries

- **Scalp Injury:** Most head injuries only damage the scalp (a cut, scrape, bruise, or swelling). It is common for children to fall and hit their head at some point while growing up. This is especially common when a child is learning to walk. Big lumps (bruises) can occur with minor injuries because there is a large blood supply to the scalp. For the same reason, small cuts on the head may bleed a lot. Bruises on the forehead sometimes cause black eyes 1 to 3 days later because the blood spreads downward by gravity.
- **Skull Fracture:** Only 1% to 2% of children with head injuries will get a skull fracture. Usually there are no other symptoms except for a headache at the site where the head was hit. Most skull fractures occur without any injury to the brain, and they heal easily.
- **Concussion:** A concussion is a mild injury to the brain that changes how the brain normally works. It is usually caused by a sudden blow or jolt to the head. Many children bump or hit their heads without causing a concussion. The most common signs of a concussion are a brief period of confusion or memory loss following the injury. Other signs of a concussion can include a headache, vomiting, dizziness, acting dazed, or being knocked out. A person does NOT need to be knocked out (lose consciousness) to have had a concussion. Following a concussion, some children have ongoing symptoms such as mild headaches, dizziness, thinking difficulties, school problems, or emotional changes for several weeks.

- **Brain injuries** are rare but are recognized by the presence of any one of the following symptoms:
  - Difficult to awaken or keep awake
  - Confused thinking and talking
  - Slurred speech
  - Weakness of arms or legs
  - Unsteady walking

When to Call Your Doctor

Call 911 Now (Your Child May Need an Ambulance) If

- A seizure (convulsion) occurred
- Knocked unconscious for longer than 1 minute
- Not moving neck normally (CAUTION: Protect the neck from any movement.)
- Difficult to awaken
- Confused thinking, slurred speech, unsteady walking, OR weakness of arms or legs present now
- Major bleeding that can't be stopped

Call Your Doctor Now (Night or Day) If

- You think your child has a serious injury
- Your child is younger than 1 year
- Neck pain
- Knocked unconscious for less than 1 minute
- Had confused thinking, slurred speech, unsteady walking, OR weakness of arms or legs, BUT fine now
- Blurred vision persists for more than 5 minutes
- Skin is split open or gaping and may need stitches
- Bleeding that won't stop after 10 minutes of direct pressure
- Large swelling (larger than 1 inch or 2.5 cm)
- Large dent in skull
- Injury caused by high speed (eg, auto accident) or blow from hard object (eg, golf club)
- Fall from a dangerous height (more than 3 feet [1 m] if child is younger than 2 years, and more than 5 feet [1.5 m] if child is older than 2 years)

- Vomited 2 or more times within 3 days of injury
- Watery fluid dripping from the nose or ear while child is not crying
- Severe headache or crying
- Can't remember what happened

Call Your Doctor Within 24 Hours (Between 9:00 am and 4:00 pm) If

- You think your child needs to be seen
- Headache persists more than 3 days

Call Your Doctor During Weekday Office Hours If

- You have other questions or concerns
- No tetanus shot in more than 5 years for DIRTY cuts (more than 10 years for CLEAN cuts)

Parent Care at Home If

- Minor head injury and you don't think your child needs to be seen

Home Care Advice for Scalp Injuries

1. **Wound Care:** If there is a scrape or cut, wash it off with soap and water. Then apply pressure with a sterile gauze for 10 minutes to stop any bleeding.
2. **Local Cold**
   - Apply a cold pack or ice bag wrapped in a wet cloth to any swelling for 20 minutes.
   - Reason: prevent big lumps ("goose eggs"). Also, reduces pain.
   - Repeat in 1 hour, then as needed.
3. **Observation:** Observe your child closely during the first 2 hours following the injury.
   - Encourage your child to lie down and rest until all symptoms have cleared (Note: mild headache, mild dizziness, and nausea are common).
   - Allow your child to sleep if he wants to, but keep him nearby.
   - Awaken after 2 hours of sleeping to check the ability to walk and talk.
4. **Diet:** Offer only clear fluids to drink, in case she vomits. Regular diet OK after 2 hours.

5. **Pain Medicine**
   - Give acetaminophen (eg, Tylenol) or ibuprofen (eg, Advil) as needed for pain relief (see dosage table in Appendix A or E).
   - EXCEPTION: Avoid until 2 hours have passed from injury without any vomiting.
   - Never give aspirin to children and teens (Reason: always increases risk of bleeding).

6. **Special Precautions at Night**
   - Mainly, sleep in the same room as your child for 2 nights.
   - Reason: if a complication occurs, you will recognize it because your child will first develop a severe headache, vomiting, confusion, or other change in behavior.
   - Optional: If you are worried, awaken your child once during the night. Check the ability to walk and talk.
   - After 48 hours, return to a normal routine.

7. **Expected Course:** Most head impact only causes a scalp injury. The swelling may take a week to resolve. The local headache at the site of impact usually clears in 2 to 3 days.

8. **Call Your Doctor If**
   - Pain or crying becomes severe.
   - Vomiting occurs 2 or more times.
   - Your child becomes difficult to awaken or confused.
   - Walking or talking becomes difficult.
   - Your child becomes worse.

And remember, contact your doctor if your child develops any of the "Call Your Doctor" symptoms.

Chapter 3

Headache

Definition

- Pain or discomfort of the scalp or forehead areas.
- The face and ears are excluded.

Causes
- **Viral Illnesses:** Most headaches are part of a viral illness, especially with colds. These usually last a few days.
- **Muscle Tension Headaches:** The most common type of recurrent headaches. Muscle tension headaches give a feeling of tightness around the head. The neck muscles also become sore and tight. Tension headaches can be caused by staying in one position for a long time, such as when reading or using a computer. Other children get tension headaches as a reaction to stress, such as pressure for better grades or family disagreements.
- **Migraine Headaches:** Recurrent severe, incapacitating headaches.
- **Other Common Causes:** Hunger, exertion, sunlight, coughing.
- **Frontal Sinusitis:** Can cause a frontal headache just above the eyebrow. Rare before 10 years of age because frontal sinus is not developed. Other sinuses cause face pain, not headache.
- **Serious Causes:** Meningitis or encephalitis. Symptoms include a headache, stiff neck, vomiting, fever, and confusion.

See More Appropriate Topic (Instead of This One) If
- Followed a head injury within last 3 days (see Chapter 2, Head Injury)
- Pain is around the eye or cheekbone (see Chapter 14, Sinus Pain or Congestion)

When to Call Your Doctor

Call 911 Now (Your Child May Need an Ambulance) If
- Difficult to awaken or passed out
- Confused thinking or talking, or slurred speech
- Blurred or double vision
- Weakness of arm or leg, or unsteady walking

Call Your Doctor Now (Night or Day) If
- Your child looks or acts very sick
- Stiff neck (can't touch chin to chest)
- Severe headache
- Vomiting

Call Your Doctor Within 24 Hours (Between 9:00 am and 4:00 pm) If
- You think your child needs to be seen
- Fever
- Sinus pain (not just congestion) of forehead

Call Your Doctor During Weekday Office Hours If
- You have other questions or concerns
- Headache without other symptoms present longer than 24 hours
- Sore throat present longer than 48 hours
- Any headache present more than 3 days
- Headaches are a recurrent chronic problem

Parent Care at Home If
- Mild headache and you don't think your child needs to be seen

Home Care Advice for Headaches

Treatment for Mild Headache

1. **Pain Medicine:** Give acetaminophen (eg, Tylenol) or ibuprofen (eg, Advil) as needed for pain relief (see dosage table in Appendix A or E). Headaches caused by fever are also helped by fever reduction.

2. **Food:** Give fruit juice or food if your child is hungry or hasn't eaten in more than 4 hours (Reason: skipping a meal can cause a headache in many children).

3. **Rest:** Lie down in a quiet place and relax until feeling better.

4. **Local Cold:** Apply a cold, wet washcloth or cold pack to the forehead for 20 minutes.

5. **Stretching:** Stretch and massage any tight neck muscles.

6. **Call Your Doctor If**
   - Headache becomes severe.
   - Vomiting occurs.
   - Isolated headache lasts longer than 24 hours.
   - Headache lasts more than 3 days.
   - Your child becomes worse.

7. **Muscle Tension Headaches: Extra Advice**
   - If something is bothering your child, help him talk about it and get it off his mind.
   - Teach your child to take breaks from activities that require sustained concentration. Encourage your child to do relaxation exercises during the breaks.
   - Teach your child the importance of getting adequate sleep.
   - If overachievement causes headaches, help your child find more balance.
   - CAUTION: Your child should have a complete medical checkup before you conclude that recurrent headaches are caused by worrying too much or stress.

Treatment for Migraine Headache

8. **Reassurance:** This headache is similar to previous migraine headaches that your child has experienced.

9. **Migraine Medication**
   - If your child's doctor has prescribed a specific medication for migraine, give it as directed as soon as the migraine starts. If not, ibuprofen (eg, Advil) is the best over-the-counter drug for migraine. Give ibuprofen now and repeat in 6 hours if needed (see dosage table in Appendix E).

10. **Sleep:** Have your child lie down in a dark, quiet place and try to fall asleep. People with migraine often awaken from sleep with their migraine gone.

11. **Call Your Doctor If**
    - Headache becomes much worse than usual.
    - Headache lasts longer than usual.

> **And remember, contact your doctor if your child develops any of the "Call Your Doctor" symptoms.**

Part 2

Eye
Symptoms

Chapter 4

Eye, Allergy

Definition

- An allergic reaction of the eyes.
- The eyes are itchy and watery.

Symptoms
- Itchy eyes with frequent rubbing
- Increased tearing (watery eyes)
- Red or pink eyes
- Mild swelling of the eyelids
- No discharge or a minimal sticky, stringy, mucus discharge
- No pain or fever

Causes
- **Pollens:** Grass, trees, weeds, molds. Pollens travel in the air.
- **Pets:** Cats, dogs, rabbits, horses. Animal allergens may be transferred to the eyes by the hands but can also be airborne.

See More Appropriate Topic (Instead of This One) If
- Runny, itchy nose and sneezing are also present (see Chapter 12, Hay Fever [Nasal Allergy])
- Yellow or green pus in eyes (see Chapter 5, Eye, Pus or Drainage)
- Doesn't look like eye allergy (see Chapter 6, Eye, Red Without Pus)

When to Call Your Doctor

Call Your Doctor Within 24 Hours (Between 9:00 am and 4:00 pm) If

- You think your child needs to be seen
- Sacs of clear fluid (blisters) on whites of eyes or inner lids
- Eyelids are swollen shut (or almost)
- Discharge on eyelids that does not clear after taking allergy medicines for 2 days

Call Your Doctor During Weekday Office Hours If

- You have other questions or concerns
- Eyes are very itchy after taking allergy medicines for 2 days
- Diagnosis of eye allergies never confirmed by your doctor

Parent Care at Home If

- Mild eye allergy and you don't think your child needs to be seen

Home Care Advice for Eye Allergy

1. **Wash Allergens Off the Face**
   - Use a wet washcloth to clean off the eyelids and surrounding face.
   - Rinse the eyes with a small amount of warm water (tears will do the rest).
   - Then apply a cold, wet washcloth to the itchy eye.
   - Wash the hair every night because it collects lots of pollen.

2. **Oral Antihistamines**
   - If the nose is also itchy and runny, your child probably has hay fever (ie, allergic symptoms of the nose AND eyes).
   - Give your child an oral antihistamine, which should relieve nose and eye symptoms.
   - Oral antihistamines usually control eye symptoms and avoid the need for eyedrops.
   - Benadryl or chlorpheniramine (CTM) products are very effective (no prescription needed). They need to be given every 6 to 8 hours (see dosage table in Appendix B or D).
   - The bedtime dosage is especially important for healing the lining of the nose.
   - Continue oral antihistamines every day until pollen season is over (usually 2 months for each pollen).

3. **New Antihistamine Eyedrops (Ketotifen) for Pollen Allergies: First Choice**
   - Usually an oral antihistamine will adequately control the allergic symptoms of the eye.
   - If the eyes remain itchy and poorly controlled, buy some ketotifen antihistamine eyedrops (no prescription needed).
   - **Dosage:** 1 drop every 12 hours.
   - Ask your pharmacist to recommend a brand (eg, Zaditor, Alaway).
   - For severe allergies, the continuous use of ketotifen eyedrops on a daily basis during pollen season will give the best control.

4. **Older Antihistamine/Vasoconstrictor Eyedrops: Second Choice**
   - Usually the eyes will feel much better after the allergic substance is washed out and cold compresses are applied.
   - If not, this type of eyedrop can be used for intermittent eye allergy symptoms (no prescription needed).
   - Ask your pharmacist to recommend a brand (eg, Naphcon-A, Opcon-A, Visine-A).
   - Avoid vasoconstrictor eyedrops without an antihistamine (without an A in the name) (Reason: they only treat the redness, not the cause).
   - **Dosage:** 1 drop every 8 hours as necessary.
   - Avoid continuous use for more than 5 days (Reason: rebound red eyes).
   - **Disadvantage:** Less effective than ketotifen eyedrops.
5. **Contacts:** Some children with contact lenses may need to switch to glasses temporarily (Reason: to permit faster healing).
6. **Expected Course:** If the allergic substance can be identified and avoided (eg, a cat), the symptoms will not recur. Most eye allergies continue through the pollen season (4 to 8 weeks).
7. **Call Your Doctor If**
   - Itchy eyes aren't controlled in 2 days with continuous allergy treatment.
   - Your child becomes worse.

> **And remember, contact your doctor if your child develops any of the "Call Your Doctor" symptoms.**

Chapter 5

Eye, Pus or Discharge

Definition

- Yellow or green discharge from a bacterial eye infection

Symptoms
- Yellow or green discharge or pus in the eye.
- Dried pus on the eyelids and eyelashes.
- The eyelashes are especially likely to be stuck (matted) together following sleep.
- The whites of the eye may or may not have some redness or pinkness.
- The eyelids are usually puffy because of irritation from the infection.

Cause
- Bacterial infection of the eye, usually on top of a cold in the eye.
- A small amount of pus (or mucus) that's only present in the corner of the eye is unimportant and usually caused by an irritant or a virus.

Return to School
- Your child can return to child care or school after using antibiotic eyedrops for 24 hours, if the pus is minimal.

See More Appropriate Topic (Instead of This One) If
- No pus in eye (see Chapter 6, Eye, Red Without Pus)
- Main symptom is itchy eyes (see Chapter 4, Eye, Allergy)

When to Call Your Doctor

Call Your Doctor Now (Night or Day) If
- Your child looks or acts very sick
- Eyelid is very red or very swollen
- Blurred vision reported
- Eye pain that's more than mild
- Cloudy spot or haziness of the cornea (clear part of the eye)
- Fever above 104°F (40°C) and not improved 2 hours after fever medicine
- Child is younger than 12 weeks with fever above 100.4°F (38.0°C) rectally (CAUTION: Do NOT give your baby any fever medicine before being seen.)

Call Your Doctor Within 24 Hours (Between 9:00 am and 4:00 pm) If
- Fever returns after gone for longer than 24 hours
- Using antibiotic eyedrops more than 3 days and pus persists
- Yellow or green discharge or pus in the eye, but none of the symptoms described herein (Reason: probably needs prescription antibiotic eyedrops to treat it)

Home Care Advice for Pus in the Eye
(Pending Talking With Your Doctor)

1. **Reassurance**
   - Bacterial eye infections are a common complication of a cold.
   - They respond to home treatment with antibiotic eyedrops, which require a prescription.
   - They are not harmful to vision.
   - Until you get some antibiotic eyedrops, do the following:
2. **Remove Pus**
   - Remove the dried and liquid pus from the eyelids with warm water and wet cotton balls.
   - Do this whenever pus is seen on the eyelids.
   - Once you have antibiotic eyedrops, they will not work unless the pus is removed each time before they are put in.
3. **Contact Lenses:** Children with contact lenses need to switch to glasses temporarily (Reason: to prevent damage to the cornea). Disinfect the contacts before wearing them again (or discard them if disposable).
4. **Contagiousness:** Your child can return to child care or school after using antibiotic eyedrops for 24 hours, if the pus is minimal. Antibiotic eyedrops can be used for other family members who develop the same symptoms.
5. **Expected Course:** With treatment, yellow discharge should clear up in 3 days. Red eyes (which are part of the underlying cold) may persist for up to a week.
6. **Call Your Doctor If**
   - Eyelid becomes red or swollen.
   - Your child becomes worse.

And remember, contact your doctor if your child develops any of the "Call Your Doctor" symptoms.

Chapter 6

Eye, Red Without Pus

Definition

- Redness or pinkness of the white of the eye and inner eyelids.
- May have increased tearing (watery eye).
- Eyelid may be puffy or mildly swollen.
- No pus or other discharge.

Causes

- **Pinkeye:** When the white of the eye (sclera) becomes pink or red, it's called pinkeye. Conjunctivitis is another name for pinkeye. The conjunctiva is the membrane that covers the white of the eye. It becomes pink when it is infected or irritated. Pinkeye has many causes.
- **Viral conjunctivitis** (part of a cold) is the main cause of pinkeye without pus.
- **Bacterial Conjunctivitis:** Pinkeye plus the eyelids are stuck together with pus. Usually this is a secondary infection of viral conjunctivitis.
- **Allergic conjunctivitis** from pollens. Most children with eye allergies also have nasal allergies (hay fever) with sneezing and clear nasal discharge.
- **Irritant conjunctivitis** from sunscreen, soap, chlorinated pool water, smoke, or smog.
- Irritants can also be transferred by touching the eye with dirty fingers (eg, food, plant resins).
- **Foreign Body:** If only one side has pinkeye, a foreign body in the eye must be considered.

Return to School

- Pinkeye with a watery discharge is harmless and mildly contagious. Children with colds in the eye usually do not need to miss any child care or school.

See More Appropriate Topic (Instead of This One) If

- Yellow or green pus in eye (see Chapter 5, Eye, Pus or Discharge)
- Main symptom is itchy eyes (see Chapter 4, Eye, Allergy)

When to Call Your Doctor

Call Your Doctor Now (Night or Day) If

- Your child looks or acts very sick
- Eyelid is very red or very swollen
- Constant tearing or blinking
- Blurred vision
- Eye pain that's more than mild
- Cloudy spot or haziness of the cornea (clear part of the eye)
- Child turns away from any light
- Child is younger than 12 weeks with fever above 100.4°F (38.0°C) rectally (CAUTION: Do NOT give your baby any fever medicine before being seen.)

Call Your Doctor Within 24 Hours (Between 9:00 am and 4:00 pm) If

- You think your child needs to be seen
- Only 1 eye is red and present longer than 24 hours
- Fever returns after gone for longer than 24 hours

Call Your Doctor During Weekday Office Hours If

- You have other questions or concerns
- Child is younger than 1 month
- Redness lasts more than 7 days

Parent Care at Home If

- Red eye is part of a cold and you don't think your child needs to be seen
- Red eye caused by mild irritant (eg, soap, sunscreen, food, smoke, smog, chlorine, perfume) and you don't think your child needs to be seen

Home Care Advice for Red Eye Without Pus

Treatment for Viral Eye Infections

1. **Reassurance:** Some viruses cause watery eyes (viral conjunctivitis). It may be the first symptom of a cold. It isn't serious and you can treat that at home. Colds can also cause a small amount of mucus to collect in the inner corner of the eye.
2. **Eye Cleansing:** Cleanse eyelids with warm water and a clean cotton ball at least every 2 hours while your child is awake and at home. This usually will keep a bacterial infection from occurring.
3. **Artificial Tears**
   - Artificial tears often make red eyes feel better (no prescription needed).
   - Use 1 drop per eye 3 times a day. Use them after cleansing the eyelids.
   - Antibiotic and vasoconstrictor eyedrops do not help viral eye infections.
4. **Contacts:** Children with contact lenses need to switch to glasses temporarily (Reason: to prevent damage to the cornea).
5. **Contagiousness**
   - Pinkeye with a watery discharge is harmless and mildly contagious.
   - Children with colds in the eye do not need to miss any child care or school.
   - Pinkeye is not a public health risk and keeping these children home is overreacting. If asked, tell the school your child is on eyedrops (artificial tears).
6. **Expected Course:** Pinkeye with a cold usually lasts about 7 days.
7. **Call Your Doctor If**
   - Yellow or green discharge develops.
   - Redness lasts more than 1 week.
   - Your child becomes worse.

Treatment for Mild Eye Irritants

1. **Reassurance:** Most eye irritants cause transient redness of the eyes. You can treat that at home.
2. **Face Cleansing:** Wash the face with mild soap and water. Wash off eyelids with water. This will remove any irritants.
3. **Eye Irrigation:** Irrigate the eye with warm water for 5 minutes.
4. **Eyedrops**
   - Red eyes from irritants usually feel much better after the irritant has been washed out.
   - If they remain uncomfortable and bloodshot, instill artificial tears or long-acting vasoconstrictor eyedrops (no prescription needed).
   - You can ask your pharmacist to recommend a brand.
   - Use 1 drop every 8 to 12 hours as necessary.
5. **Expected Course:** After removal of the irritant, the eyes usually return to normal color in 1 to 2 hours.
6. **Prevention:** Try to avoid future exposure to the irritant.
7. **Call Your Doctor If**
   - Your child develops yellow or green pus in the eye.
   - Redness lasts more than 7 days.
   - Your child becomes worse.

> **And remember, contact your doctor if your child develops any of the "Call Your Doctor" symptoms.**

Part 3

Ear
Symptoms

Chapter 7

Ear, Discharge

Definition

- Drainage of substances or liquids with varied colors and consistency from the ear canal.
- Drainage through an ear tube is included.

Causes

- **Normal Discharge:** Earwax or water. Earwax is light brown, dark brown, or orange brown in color.
- **Abnormal Discharge:** Cloudy fluid or pus. Main cause is an ear infection with drainage from a ruptured eardrum or through a ventilation tube.

When to Call Your Doctor

Call Your Doctor Now (Night or Day) If

- Your child looks or acts very sick
- Pink or red swelling behind the ear
- Clear or bloody fluid following head injury
- Bleeding from the ear canal (EXCEPTION: few drops and follows ear examination)
- Fever above 104°F (40°C) and not improved 2 hours after fever medicine

Call Your Doctor Within 24 Hours (Between 9:00 am and 4:00 pm) If

- You think your child needs to be seen
- Ear pain or unexplained crying
- Discharge is yellow or green, cloudy white, or foul smelling (pus)
- Clear drainage (not from a head injury) persists longer than 24 hours

Call Your Doctor During Weekday Office Hours If

- You have other questions or concerns

Parent Care at Home If

- Probably normal earwax or other harmless discharge and you don't think your child needs to be seen

Home Care Advice for Ear Discharge

1. **Earwax**
   - Earwax protects the lining of the ear canal and has germ-killing properties.
   - If the earwax is removed, the ear canals become itchy.
   - Do not use cotton swabs (Q-tips) in your child's ear.
   - Call your doctor if it begins to look like pus (yellow or green discharge).

2. **Clear Discharge (Without Head Trauma)**
   - It's probably tears or water that entered the ear canal during a bath, shower, swimming, or water fight.
   - Don't overlook ear drops your child or someone else used without telling you.
   - In children with ventilation tubes, some clear or slightly cloudy fluid can occur when a temporary tube blockage opens up and drains.
   - Call your doctor if clear drainage persists for more than 24 hours or recurs.

3. **Blood After Ear Examination**
   - If your doctor had to remove earwax to see the eardrum, about 10% of the time this causes a small scratch to the lining of the ear canal. Usually the scratch oozes 1 or 2 drops of blood and then clots.
   - This should heal up completely in a few days.
   - It shouldn't affect hearing.
   - Don't put anything in the ear canal because it will probably restart the bleeding.
   - Call your doctor if bleeding continues or recurs.

4. **Suspected Ear Infection:** Cloudy fluid or pus draining from the ear canal almost always means there's a small tear in the eardrum and a middle ear infection. Give acetaminophen (eg, Tylenol) or ibuprofen (eg, Advil) as needed for pain relief until the office visit (see Chapter 9, Earache, for details).

5. **Call Your Doctor If**
   - Your child becomes worse.

And remember, contact your doctor if your child develops any of the "Call Your Doctor" symptoms.

Chapter 8

Ear, Pulling at or Itchy

Definition

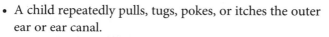

- A child repeatedly pulls, tugs, pokes, or itches the outer ear or ear canal.
- No crying or report of earache.

Causes

- **Main Cause (Infants):** Normal touching and pulling with discovery of ears. This behavior is usually not seen before 4 months of age.
- **Main Cause (Older Children):** Mild swimmer's ear from (1) water accumulation during swimming or showers, (2) soap or shampoo retention, or (3) canal irritation from cotton-tipped swabs. Some children are reacting to a piece of earwax in the ear canal.
- **Not an Ear Infection:** Most younger children (younger than 2 or 3 years) who pull or poke at the ear are unable to confirm or deny the presence of an earache. Dr Ray Baker examined 100 children with ear pulling as the chief complaint. The main conclusion was that simple ear pulling without other symptoms of an illness or infection was never associated with ear infections.

See More Appropriate Topic (Instead of This One) If

- Child is mainly crying and not pulling at ears (see Chapter 1, Crying)
- Child reports earache (see Chapter 9, Earache)

When to Call Your Doctor

Call Your Doctor Now (Night or Day) If

- Your child looks or acts very sick
- Fever above 104°F (40°C) and not improved 2 hours after fever medicine
- Child is younger than 12 weeks with fever above 100.4°F (38.0°C) rectally (CAUTION: Do NOT give your baby any fever medicine before being seen.)

Call Your Doctor Within 24 Hours (Between 9:00 am and 4:00 pm) If

- You think your child needs to be seen
- Seems to be in pain or crying without an obvious reason
- Starts waking from sleep
- Fever or symptoms of a cold are present
- Drainage from the ear canal
- Constant digging inside 1 ear canal

Call Your Doctor During Weekday Office Hours If

- You have other questions or concerns
- Pulling at the ear continues more than 3 days
- Itching continues more than 1 week

Parent Care at Home If

- Normal ear touching or pulling
- Itchy ear canal

Home Care Advice for Ear-pulling Habit or Itchy Ear Canal

1. **Reassurance**
   - Most of these children have discovered their ears and are playing with them.
   - Some have an itchy ear canal.
   - Ear pulling that is a new symptom and begins when a child has a cold usually is caused by fluid in the middle ear. Less often it's caused by an ear infection.
   - Ear pulling without other symptoms is not a sign of an ear infection.

2. **Habit:** If touching the ear is a new habit, ignore it (prevent doing it for attention).

3. **White Vinegar Ear Drops**
   - For itchy ear canal, use half-strength white vinegar by diluting it with equal parts water.
   - Place 2 drops in each ear canal daily for 3 days (Reason: restore the normal acid pH).
   - EXCEPTION: ear drainage, ear tubes, or hole in eardrum.

4. **Avoid Soap:** Keep soap and shampoo out of the ear canal.

5. **Avoid Cotton Swabs:** Cotton swabs remove the earwax that normally protects the lining of the ear canal, and this leads to itching and irritation.

6. **Expected Course:** With this treatment, most itching is gone in 2 or 3 days.

7. **Call Your Doctor If**
   - Pulling at the ear continues for more than 3 days.
   - Itching of ear continues for more than 1 week.
   - Your child becomes worse.

And remember, contact your doctor if your child develops any of the "Call Your Doctor" symptoms.

Chapter 9

Earache

Definition

- Pain or discomfort in or around the ear.
- Child reports an earache.
- Younger child acts like she did with previous ear infection (eg, crying, fussy).

Cause

- Usually due to an ear infection.
- Ear infections can be caused by viruses or bacteria. Usually, your child's doctor can tell the difference by looking at the eardrum.
- Ear infections peak at ages 6 months to 2 years.
- The onset of ear infections peaks on day 3 of a cold.

Return to School

- An earache or ear infection is not contagious. There is no need to miss any school or child care.

When to Call Your Doctor

Call 911 Now (Your Child May Need an Ambulance) If

- Not moving or very weak

Call Your Doctor Now (Night or Day) If

- Your child looks or acts very sick
- Earache is severe and not improved 2 hours after taking ibuprofen (eg, Advil)
- Pink or red swelling behind the ear
- Stiff neck (can't touch chin to chest)
- Pointed object was inserted into the ear canal (eg, pencil, stick, wire)
- Weak immune system (eg, sickle cell disease, HIV, chemotherapy, organ transplant, chronic steroids)
- Fever above 104°F (40°C) and not improved 2 hours after fever medicine

Call Your Doctor Within 24 Hours (Between 9:00 am and 4:00 pm) If

- Earache, but none of the symptoms described previously (Reason: possible ear infection)
- Pus or cloudy discharge from ear canal

Home Care Advice for Suspected Ear Infection
(Until Your Child Can Be Seen)

1. **Reassurance**
   - Your child may have an ear infection. The only way to be sure is to examine the eardrum.
   - Diagnosis and treatment can safely wait until morning if the earache begins after your child's doctor's office is closed.
   - Ear pain can be controlled with pain medicine and ear drops.
2. **Pain or Fever Medicine:** Give acetaminophen (eg, Tylenol) or ibuprofen (eg, Advil) as needed for pain relief or fever above 102°F (39°C) (see dosage table in Appendix A or E).
3. **Local Cold:** Apply a cold pack or a cold, wet washcloth to the outer ear for 20 minutes to reduce pain while the pain medicine takes effect (Note: some children prefer local heat for 20 minutes).
4. **Ear Drainage**
   - If pus or cloudy fluid is draining from the ear canal, the eardrum has ruptured from an ear infection.
   - Wipe the pus away as it appears.
   - Avoid plugging with cotton (Reason: retained pus causes irritation or infection of the ear canal).
5. **Ear Drops:** 3 drops of olive oil (or prescription ear drops) will usually relieve pain not helped by pain medicine. If your child has ear tubes or a hole in the eardrum, don't use them.
6. **Contagiousness:** Ear infections are not contagious.
7. **Call Your Doctor If**
   - Your child develops severe pain.
   - Your child becomes worse.

> **And remember, contact your doctor if your child develops any of the "Call Your Doctor" symptoms.**

Chapter 10

Ear Infection Questions

Definition

- Your child was recently examined and diagnosed as having a middle ear infection.
- You are concerned that your child's fever, earache, or other symptom is not improving fast enough.
- Your child is still taking an antibiotic for the ear infection.

Ear Infections (Otitis Media)

- **Definition:** An infection of the middle ear (the space behind the eardrum).
- **Cause:** Blocked eustachian tube, usually as part of a common cold. The eustachian tube connects the middle ear to the back of the nose. Blockage results in middle ear fluid (viral otitis). If the fluid becomes superinfected (bacterial otitis), the fluid turns to pus, the eardrum bulges, and pain increases.
- Ear infections peak at ages 6 months to 2 years. They are a common problem until age 8 years.
- The onset of ear infections peaks on day 3 of a cold.
- **Prevalence:** 90% of children have at least 1 ear infection. Repeated ear infections occur in 20% of children. Ear infections are the most common bacterial infection of childhood.

Symptoms

- The main symptom is an earache.
- Younger children will cry, act fussy, or have difficulty sleeping because of the pain.
- About 50% of children with an ear infection will have a fever.
- **Complication:** In 5% to 10% of children, the pressure in the middle ear causes the eardrum to rupture and drain cloudy fluid or pus. This small hole usually heals over in 2 or 3 days.

Return to School

- An earache or ear infection is not contagious. Your child should stay home only until any fever is resolved.

When to Call Your Doctor

Call 911 Now (Your Child May Need an Ambulance) If

- Not moving or very weak

Call Your Doctor Now (Night or Day) If

- Your child looks or acts very sick
- Stiff neck (can't touch chin to chest)
- Walking is unsteady
- Fever above 104°F (40°C) and not improved 2 hours after fever medicine
- Pain is severe and not improved 2 hours after ibuprofen (eg, Advil)
- Crying is inconsolable and not improved 2 hours after ibuprofen (eg, Advil)
- New-onset pink or red swelling behind the ear
- Crooked smile (weakness of 1 side of face)
- New onset of vomiting (EXCEPTION: Vomiting follows hard coughing.)

Call Your Doctor Within 24 Hours (Between 9:00 am and 4:00 pm) If

- You think your child needs to be seen
- Taking antibiotic longer than 48 hours and fever persists or recurs
- Taking antibiotic more than 3 days and ear pain not improved or recurs
- Taking antibiotic more than 3 days and ear discharge persists or recurs

Call Your Doctor During Weekday Office Hours If

- You have other questions or concerns

Parent Care at Home If

- Ear infection with no complications and you don't think your child needs to be seen
- Hearing loss with an ear infection
- Prevention of ear infections
- Ear tube surgery questions

Home Care Advice for Ear Infection

Treatment for an Ear Infection

1. **Reassurance**
   - Most ear infections do not respond to the first dose of antibiotic.
   - Often there is no improvement the first day.
   - Children gradually get better over 2 to 3 days.
   - Note: for mild ear infections in children older than 2 years, antibiotics may not be needed.
2. **Continue the Antibiotic**
   - The antibiotic will kill the bacteria that are causing the ear infection.
   - Try not to forget any of the doses.
   - Give the antibiotic until the bottle is empty (or all pills are gone) (Reason: prevent the ear infection from flaring up again).
3. **Pain or Fever Medicine:** Give acetaminophen (eg, Tylenol) or ibuprofen (eg, Advil) as needed for pain relief or fever above 102°F (39°C) (see dosage table in Appendix A or E).
4. **Local Cold:** Apply a cold pack or a cold, wet washcloth to outer ear for 20 minutes to reduce pain while medicine takes effect (Note: some children prefer local heat for 20 minutes) (CAUTION: Hot or cold pack applied too long could cause burn or frostbite).
5. **Ear Drops:** 3 drops of prescription ear drops or olive oil drops will usually relieve pain not helped by pain medicine. If your child has ear tubes or a hole in the eardrum, don't use them.
6. **Restrictions**
   - Your child can go outside and does not need to cover her ears.
   - Swimming is fine as long as there is no perforation (tear) in the eardrum or drainage from the ear.
   - Children with ear infections can travel safely by aircraft if they are taking antibiotics. Most will not have any increase in ear pain while flying.
   - Give your child a dose of ibuprofen (eg, Advil) 1 hour before takeoff to deal with any discomfort he might have. Also, during descent (prior to landing), have your child swallow fluids, suck on a pacifier, or chew gum.

7. **Contagiousness:** Your child can return to school or child care when feeling better and any fever is gone. Ear infections are not contagious.
8. **Expected Course:** If you give your child antibiotic as directed, the fever should be gone by 2 days (48 hours). The earache should be improved by 2 days and gone by 3 days (72 hours).
9. **Ear Discharge**
   - If pus or cloudy fluid is draining from the ear canal, it means the eardrum has a small tear in it caused by pressure from the ear infection. It also normally occurs if your child has ear tubes.
   - The pus may be blood tinged.
   - This usually heals nicely after the ear infection is treated.
   - Wipe the discharge away as it appears.
   - Avoid plugging the ear canal with cotton (Reason: retained pus can cause infection of the lining of the ear canal).
10. **Call Your Doctor If**
   - Fever lasts more than 2 days on antibiotics.
   - Ear pain becomes severe or crying becomes inconsolable.
   - Ear pain lasts more than 3 days on antibiotics.
   - Ear discharge is not improved after 3 days on antibiotics.
   - Your child becomes worse.

Treatment for Hearing Loss With an Ear Infection

1. **Temporary Hearing Loss**
   - During an ear infection, fluid builds up in the middle ear space instead of draining out normally to the back of the nose.
   - The fluid can cause a temporary mild hearing loss.
   - It will gradually improve and should resolve with antibiotic treatment.
   - In some children, it may take longer for fluid to go away, even though the fluid is no longer infected. In 90% of children, it clears up by itself over 1 to 2 months.
   - Permanent damage to hearing from ear infections is very rare.
2. **Talking With Your Child**
   - Get close to your child and get eye contact.
   - Speak in a louder voice than you normally use.
   - Reduce any background noise from radio or TV while talking with your child.

3. **Call Your Doctor If**
   - Hearing loss not improved after the antibiotic course is finished.

Prevention of Recurrent Ear Infections

1. **Reassurance:** Some children have recurrent ear infections. If your child has lots of ear infections, here are some ways to prevent future ones.
2. **Avoid Tobacco Smoke:** Protect your child from tobacco smoke because it increases the frequency and severity of ear infections. Be sure no one smokes in your home or at child care.
3. **Avoid Excessive Colds**
   - Most ear infections start with a cold. Reduce your child's exposure to children with colds during the first year of life.
   - Try to delay the use of large child care centers during the first year by using a sitter in your home or a small home-based child care.
4. **Breastfeed**
   - Breastfeed your baby during the first 6 to 12 months of life.
   - Antibodies in breast milk reduce the rate of ear infections.
   - If you are breastfeeding, continue.
   - If you are not, consider it with your next child.
5. **Avoid Bottle Propping**
   - During feedings, hold your baby with his head higher than his stomach.
   - Feeding in the horizontal position can cause formula to flow back into the eustachian tube.
   - Allowing an infant to hold his own bottle can cause milk to drain into the middle ear.
6. **Get All Recommended Immunizations:** The pneumococcal and flu vaccines will protect your child from serious diseases and some ear infections.
7. **Control Allergies:** If your infant has a continuously runny nose, consider allergy as a contributing factor to the ear infections. If your child has other allergies such as eczema, your child's doctor can check for a milk protein or soy protein allergy.

8. **Evaluate Any Snoring:** If your toddler snores every night or breathes through her mouth, she may have large adenoids. Large adenoids can contribute to ear infections. Talk to your child's doctor about this.

Ear Tube Surgery Questions

1. **Ventilation Tubes**
   - Ventilation tubes are tiny plastic tubes that are inserted through the eardrum by an ear, nose, and throat surgeon.
   - The tubes allow fluid to drain out of the middle ear space and air to reenter.
   - This reduces the risk of recurrent ear infections and returns hearing to normal.

2. **Indications for Ventilation Tubes**
   - Fluid has been present in the middle ear continuously for more than 4 months and both ears have fluid.
   - In addition, the fluid has caused a documented hearing loss greater than 20 decibels. The reason to test hearing first is that some children with fluid in their ears have nearly normal hearing and tubes are not needed.
   - A separate indication is for frequent ear infections or ear infections that do not clear up after trying multiple antibiotics.
   - Prevention techniques should be attempted before turning to surgery.
   - Discuss possible indication for ear tube with your child's doctor.

3. **Expected Course**
   - Normally the tubes come out and fall into the ear canal after about a year. Then they come out of the ear canal with the normal movement of earwax.
   - If the tubes remain in the eardrum for more than 2 years, the surgeon may need to remove them.

4. Risks of Ventilation Tubes

- After the tubes come out, they may leave scars on the eardrum or a small hole that doesn't heal. Both of these problems can cause a small hearing loss.
- Because of these possible complications and the need to give anesthesia to young children before the operation, physicians recommend ventilation tubes only for children who really need them.

> **And remember, contact your doctor if your child develops any of the "Call Your Doctor" symptoms.**

Part 4

Nose
Symptoms

Chapter 11

Colds

Definition

- Viral infection of the nose and throat

Symptoms

- Runny or congested nose.
- The nasal discharge may be clear, cloudy, yellow, or green.
- Usually associated with fever.
- A sore throat often is the first symptom.
- Sometimes associated with a cough, hoarse voice, watery eyes, and swollen lymph nodes in the neck.

Cause

- Colds are caused by several respiratory viruses. Healthy children average 6 colds a year. Influenza usually feels like a bad cold with more fever and muscle aches.
- Colds are not serious. Between 5% and 10% of children develop a bacterial complication (ear or sinus infection).

Colds: Normal Viral Symptoms

- Colds cause nasal discharge, nasal congestion, sinus congestion, ear congestion, sore throats, hoarse voice, coughs, croup, and red, watery eyes. When you combine all these symptoms, colds are the most common reason for calls to the doctor.
- Cold symptoms are also the number one reason for office and emergency department visits. Hopefully, this information will save you time and money and help you avoid some unnecessary trips to the doctor. You can be reassured the following are normal cold symptoms and children with these symptoms don't need to be seen:
  - Fever up to 3 days
  - Sore throat up to 5 days (with other cold symptoms)
  - Nasal discharge and congestion up to 2 weeks
  - Cough up to 3 weeks

Colds: Symptoms of Secondary Bacterial Infections

- Using this chapter, you can see if your child is one of the 5% to 10% of children who have ear infections or sinus infections. Many are identified with specific symptoms and patterns. Some are suspected because symptoms last too long.
  - Earache or ear discharge
  - Sinus pain not relieved by nasal washes
  - Difficulty breathing or rapid breathing
  - Fever present more than 3 days
  - Fever that goes away for 24 hours and then returns
  - Sore throat present more than 5 days
  - Nasal discharge present more than 2 weeks
  - Cough present more than 3 weeks

Return to School

- Your child can return to child care or school after the fever is gone and your child feels well enough to participate in normal activities. For practical purposes, the spread of colds cannot be prevented.

See More Appropriate Topic (Instead of This One) If

- Runny nose caused by allergies (see Chapter 12, Hay Fever [Nasal Allergy])
- Cough is the main symptom (see Chapter 23, Cough)
- Yellow or green eye discharge (see Chapter 5, Eye, Pus or Discharge)
- Child older than 5 years and pain around the eye or over the cheekbone (see Chapter 14, Sinus Pain or Congestion)

When to Call Your Doctor

Call 911 Now (Your Child May Need an Ambulance) If
- Severe difficulty breathing (struggling for each breath, unable to speak or cry because of difficulty breathing, making grunting noises with each breath)

Call Your Doctor Now (Night or Day) If
- Your child looks or acts very sick
- Not alert when awake
- Difficulty breathing not relieved by cleaning out the nose
- Weak immune system (eg, sickle cell disease, HIV, chemotherapy, organ transplant, chronic steroids)
- Fever above 104°F (40°C) and not improved 2 hours after fever medicine
- Child is younger than 12 weeks with fever above 100.4°F (38.0°C) rectally (CAUTION: Do NOT give your baby any fever medicine before being seen.)

Call Your Doctor Within 24 Hours (Between 9:00 am and 4:00 pm) If
- You think your child needs to be seen
- Earache or cloudy discharge from ear canal
- Yellow or green eye discharge
- Sinus pain around cheekbone or eyes (not just congestion)
- Fever present for more than 3 days
- Fever returns after gone for 24 hours

Call Your Doctor During Weekday Office Hours If
- You have other questions or concerns
- Blocked nose interferes with sleep after using nasal washes several times
- Yellow scabs around the nasal openings (apply antibiotic ointment)
- Sore throat present more than 5 days
- Nasal discharge present more than 14 days

Parent Care at Home If
- Mild cold with no complications and you don't think your child needs to be seen

Home Care Advice for Colds

1. **Reassurance**
   - Because there are so many viruses that cause colds, it's normal for healthy children to get at least 6 colds a year. With every new cold, your child's body builds up immunity to that virus.
   - Most parents know when their child has a cold, often because they have it too or other children in child care or school have it. You don't need to call or see your child's doctor for common colds unless your child develops a possible complication (eg, earache).
   - The average cold lasts about 2 weeks and there isn't any medicine to make it go away sooner.
   - However, there are good ways to relieve many of the symptoms. With most colds, the initial symptom is a runny nose, followed in 3 or 4 days by a congested nose. The treatment for each is different.

2. **For a Runny Nose With Profuse Discharge: Blow or Suction the Nose**
   - The nasal mucus and discharge are washing viruses and bacteria out of the nose and sinuses.
   - Blowing the nose is all that's needed.
   - For younger children, gently suction the nose with a suction bulb.
   - Apply petroleum jelly to the nasal openings to protect them from irritation (cleanse the skin first).

3. **Nasal Washes to Open a Blocked Nose**
   - Use saline nose drops or spray to loosen up the dried mucus. If not available, you can use warm tap water.
   - **Step 1:** Instill 3 drops per nostril (if child is younger than 1 year, use 1 drop and do 1 side at a time).
   - **Step 2:** Blow (or suction) each nostril separately while closing off the other nostril. Then do other side.
   - **Step 3:** Repeat nose drops and blowing (or suctioning) until the discharge is clear.

- **Frequency:** Do nasal washes whenever your child can't breathe through her nose.
- Saline nasal sprays can be purchased without a prescription.
- Saline nose drops can also be made—add ½ teaspoon (2 mL) of table salt to 1 cup (8 oz or 240 mL) of warm water.
- Reason for nose drops: suction or nose blowing alone can't remove dried or sticky mucus.
- **Another Option:** Use a warm shower to loosen mucus. Breathe in the moist air, then blow each nostril.
- For young children, you can also use a wet cotton swab to remove sticky mucus.
- **Importance for a Young Infant:** Can't nurse or drink from a bottle unless the nose is open.

4. **Fluids:** Encourage your child to drink adequate fluids to prevent dehydration. This will also thin out nasal secretions and loosen any phlegm in the lungs.

5. **Humidifier:** If the air in your home is dry, use a humidifier.

6. **Medicines for Colds**
   - **Cold medicines** are not recommended at any age. (Reason: they are not helpful. They can't remove dried mucus from the nose. Nasal washes can.)
   - **Antihistamines** are not helpful, unless your child also has nasal allergies.
   - **Decongestants:** Over-the-counter oral decongestants (pseudoephedrine or phenylephrine) are not recommended. Although they may reduce nasal congestion in some children, they also can have side effects.
   - **Age Limit:** Before 4 years, never use any cough or cold medicines (Reason: unsafe and not approved by Food and Drug Administration). (Avoid multi-ingredient products at any age.)
   - **No Antibiotics:** Antibiotics are not helpful, unless your child develops an ear or sinus infection.

7. **Treatment for Associated Symptoms of Colds**
   - **Fever or Pain:** Use acetaminophen (eg, Tylenol) or ibuprofen (eg, Advil) for muscle aches, headaches, or fever above 102°F (39°C).
   - **Sore Throat:** Use warm chicken broth if child is older than 1 year and suck on hard candy if child is older than 6 years.
   - **Cough:** Give ½ to 1 teaspoon (2 to 5 mL) of honey for children older than 1 year, and use cough drops for children older than 6 years.
   - **Red Eyes:** Rinse eyelids frequently with wet cotton balls.

8. **Contagiousness:** Your child can return to child care or school after the fever is gone and your child feels well enough to participate in normal activities. For practical purposes, the spread of colds cannot be prevented.

9. **Expected Course:** For fever, 2 to 3 days; for nasal discharge, 7 to 14 days; for cough, 2 to 3 weeks.

10. **Call Your Doctor If**
    - Earache suspected.
    - Fever lasts more than 3 days.
    - Any fever occurs if child is younger than 12 weeks.
    - Nasal discharge lasts more than 14 days.
    - Cough lasts more than 3 weeks.
    - Your child becomes worse.

11. **Air Travel With Colds: Extra Advice**
    - It's safe to fly when your child has a cold.
    - He could develop temporary ear congestion or earache, but that's often preventable.
    - It's unusual to develop an ear infection, unless your child already is prone to frequent ear infections. However, that's not a reason to avoid flying.

12. **Prevention of Ear Congestion During Air Travel: Extra Advice**
    - Most symptoms occur during descent of the aircraft (the 15 minutes before landing).
    - Stay awake during takeoff and descent.
    - Swallow during descent using fluids or a pacifier.
    - Children older than 4 years can chew gum during descent.
    - Yawning during descent also can open the middle ear.
    - Stay well hydrated throughout the flight to prevent nasal secretions from drying out.

> **And remember, contact your doctor if your child develops any of the "Call Your Doctor" symptoms.**

Chapter 12

Hay Fever (Nasal Allergy)

Definition

- An allergic reaction of the nose (allergic rhinitis).
- An itchy nose and clear discharge are common.

Symptoms
- Clear nasal discharge with sneezing, sniffing, and nasal itching.
- Eye allergies (itchy, red, watery, and puffy) are commonly associated.
- Ear and sinus congestion may also be associated.
- A tickling, scratchy sensation in the back of the throat can be associated.
- Itchy ear canals, itchy skin, and hoarse voice are also seen.
- Symptoms occur during pollen season.
- Similar symptoms during the same month of the previous year.
- No fever.

Causes
- Hay fever is an allergic reaction of the nose and sinuses to an inhaled substance, usually a pollen.
- Grass, trees, and weeds are the most common pollens.
- Allergens from cats, dogs, horses, rabbits, and other animals.

See More Appropriate Topic (Instead of This One) If
- Doesn't look like hay fever (see Chapter 11, Colds)

When to Call Your Doctor

Call Your Doctor Within 24 Hours (Between 9:00 am and 4:00 pm) If
- You think your child needs to be seen
- Lots of coughing
- Sinus pain around cheekbone or eyes (not just congestion) and not relieved by antihistamines

Call Your Doctor During Weekday Office Hours If
- You have other questions or concerns
- Hay fever symptoms interfere with school or normal activities after taking antihistamines for 2 days
- Diagnosis of hay fever has never been confirmed by your doctor
- Year-round symptoms of nasal allergies

Parent Care at Home If
- Hay fever and you don't think your child needs to be seen

Home Care Advice for Hay Fever

1. **Reassurance**
   - Hay fever is very common, occurring in 15% of children.
   - Nose and eye symptoms can be brought under control by giving antihistamines.
   - Because pollens are in the air every day during pollen season, antihistamines must be given daily for 2 months or longer.
2. **Antihistamines**
   - Antihistamines are the drug of choice for nasal allergies.
   - Antihistamines will reduce runny nose, nasal itching, and sneezing.
   - Benadryl or chlorpheniramine (CTM) products are very effective and no prescription is needed. They need to be given every 6 to 8 hours (see dosage table in Appendix B or D).
   - The bedtime dosage is especially important for healing the lining of the nose.
   - The key to hay fever control is to give antihistamines every day during pollen season.
3. **Cetirizine (Zyrtec) or Loratadine (Claritin)**
   - Loratadine and cetirizine are nonprescription, long-acting antihistamines.
   - **Advantage:** They cause less sedation than older antihistamines (Benadryl and chlorpheniramine) AND are long-acting (last up to 24 hours).
   - **Dosage**
     - For children aged 2 to 6 years, discuss with your child's doctor first. If approved, give 2.5 mg (2.5 mL or ½ teaspoon) of liquid syrup.
     - For children aged 6 to 12 years, give a 5-mg chewable tablet once daily in the morning.
     - For children older than 12 years, give a 10-mg tablet once daily in the morning.
   - **Indication:** Drowsiness from older antihistamines interferes with function.
   - **Limitation:** Don't control hay fever symptoms as well as older antihistamines. Also, child will occasionally have breakthrough symptoms before 24 hours.
   - **Cost:** Ask pharmacist for store brand (Reason: costs less than Claritin or Zyrtec brand).

4. **Nasal Washes to Wash Out Pollen**
   - Use saline nose drops or spray to wash out pollen or to loosen up dried mucus. If not available, you can use warm tap water. Teens can just splash warm tap water in the nose and then blow.
   - **Step 1:** Instill 3 drops per nostril.
   - **Step 2:** Blow each nostril separately while closing off the other nostril. Then do other side.
   - **Step 3:** Repeat nose drops and blowing until the discharge is clear.
   - **Frequency:** Do nasal washes whenever your child can't breathe through the nose or it's very itchy.
   - Saline nasal sprays can be purchased without a prescription.
   - Saline nose drops can also be made—add ½ teaspoon (2 mL) of table salt to 1 cup (8 oz or 240 mL) of warm water.
   - **Another Option:** Use a warm shower to loosen mucus. Breathe in the moist air, then blow each nostril.
5. **Eye Allergies**
   - For eye symptoms, wash the pollen or other allergic substance off the face and eyelids.
   - Then apply cold compresses.
   - Usually an oral antihistamine will adequately control eye allergy symptoms, but sometimes eyedrops are also needed.
   - **Antihistamine Eyedrops: Ketotifen (First Choice)**
     - Ketotifen eyedrops are a safe and effective product (eg, Zaditor, Alaway) (no prescription needed).
     - **Dosage:** 1 drop every 12 hours.
     - For severe allergies, the continuous use of ketotifen eyedrops on a daily basis during pollen season will give the best control.
   - **Antihistamine/Vasoconstrictive Eyedrops (Second Choice)**
     - **Dosage:** 1 drop every 8 hours.
     - Ask your pharmacist to recommend a brand (eg, Naphcon-A, Opcon-A, Visine-A).
     - **Disadvantage:** Less effective than ketotifen eyedrops.
6. **Wash Pollen Off Body:** Remove pollen from the hair and skin with hair washing and a shower, especially before bedtime.

7. **Expected Course:** Because pollen allergies recur each year, learn to control the symptoms.
8. **Pollen Avoidance**
   - Pollen is carried in the air.
   - Keep windows closed in the home, at least in child's bedroom.
   - Keep windows closed in car, turn air-conditioning on recirculate.
   - Avoid window fans or attic fans.
   - Try to stay indoors on windy days (Reason: the pollen count is much higher when it's dry and windy).
   - Avoid playing with outdoor dog (Reason: pollen collects in the fur).
9. **Call Your Doctor If**
   - Symptoms aren't controlled in 2 days with continuous antihistamines.
   - Your child becomes worse.

And remember, contact your doctor if your child develops any of the "Call Your Doctor" symptoms.

Chapter 13

Nosebleed

Definition

- Bleeding from 1 or both nostrils
- No known injury

Causes

- Nosebleeds are common because of the rich blood supply of the nose. Common causes include
  - Dryness of the nasal lining (eg, from forced air furnace in winter).
  - Antihistamines (Reason: they also dry the nose).
  - Vigorous nose blowing.
  - Ibuprofen (eg, Advil) and aspirin (Reason: increase bleeding tendency).
  - Suctioning the nose can sometimes cause bleeding.
  - Picking or rubbing the nose.
  - Predisposing factors that make the nasal lining more fragile (eg, nasal allergies, colds, sinus infections).

When to Call Your Doctor

Call 911 Now (Your Child May Need an Ambulance) If

- Fainted or too weak to stand

Call Your Doctor Now (Night or Day) If

- You think your child has a serious injury
- Bleeding does not stop after 10 minutes of direct pressure applied correctly and tried twice
- New skin bruises or bleeding gums not caused by an injury are also present
- Large amount of blood has been lost

Call Your Doctor Within 24 Hours (Between 9:00 am and 4:00 pm) If

- You think your child needs to be seen

Call Your Doctor During Weekday Office Hours If

- You have other questions or concerns
- Child is younger than 1 year
- New-onset nosebleeds are occurring frequently
- Hard-to-stop nosebleeds are a recurrent chronic problem
- Easy bleeding present in other family members

Parent Care at Home If

- Mild nosebleed and you don't think your child needs to be seen

Home Care Advice for Nosebleed

1. **Reassurance**
   - Nosebleeds are common.
   - You should be able to stop the bleeding if you use the correct technique.
2. **Apply Pressure**
   - Gently squeeze the soft parts of the lower nose against the center wall for 10 minutes. This should apply continuous pressure to the bleeding point.
   - Use the thumb and index finger in a pinching manner.
   - If the bleeding continues, move your point of pressure.
   - Have your child sit up and breathe through the mouth during this procedure.
   - If it re-bleeds, use the same technique again.
3. **Insert Gauze**
   - If pressure alone fails, insert a gauze wet with a few decongestant nose drops (eg, nonprescription Afrin) (Reason: the gauze helps to apply pressure and nose drops shrink the blood vessels).
   - If not available or your child is younger than 1 year, use petroleum jelly applied to gauze.
   - Repeat the process of gently squeezing the lower soft parts of the nose for 10 minutes.
4. **Prevent Recurrent Nosebleeds**
   - If the air in your home is dry, use a humidifier to keep the nose from drying out.
   - Apply petroleum jelly to the center wall of the nose twice a day to promote healing.
   - For nose blowing, blow gently.
   - For nose suctioning, don't put the suction tip very far inside. Also, move it gently.
   - Avoid aspirin and ibuprofen (eg, Advil) (Reason: increase bleeding tendency).

5. **Expected Course:** More than 99% of nosebleeds will stop following 10 minutes of direct pressure if you press on the right spot. After swallowing blood from a nosebleed, your child may vomit a little blood or pass a dark stool tomorrow.

6. **Call Your Doctor If**
   - Unable to stop bleeding with 20 minutes of direct pressure.
   - Your child becomes worse.

And remember, contact your doctor if your child develops any of the "Call Your Doctor" symptoms.

Chapter 14

Sinus Pain or Congestion

Definition

- A sensation of fullness, pressure, or pain on the face overlying a sinus cavity.
- The sinuses are located above the eyebrow, behind the eye, around the eye, and over the cheekbone.

Symptoms

- The pain or pressure usually is just on one side of the face.
- Puffiness or swelling around just one eye.
- Commonly associated symptoms are a congested nose, blocked nose, nasal discharge, or postnasal sinus drip.
- Less common symptoms are bad breath, mouth breathing, sore throat from postnasal drip, and throat clearing.
- **Age Limitation:** Sinus pain is not a reliable symptom before 5 years of age.

Causes of Sinus Congestion

- **Viral Sinusitis:** Part of the common cold. Viral inflammation of the lining of the nose also involves the lining of all the sinuses.
- **Bacterial Sinusitis:** A complication in which viral sinusitis becomes secondarily infected with bacteria (occurs in 5% of colds). Main symptoms are increased sinus pain, the return of fever, or the overlying skin (around the eyelids or cheeks) becomes red or swollen. In younger children, the main symptoms are thick nasal secretions that last longer than 14 days or return of fever.
- **Allergic Sinusitis:** Sinus congestion commonly occurs with nasal allergies (eg, from pollens). Associated sneezing, itchy nose, and clear nasal discharge point to this cause.

Treatment of Sinusitis

- **Viral Sinusitis:** Nasal washes with saline. Antibiotics are not helpful.
- **Bacterial Sinusitis:** Oral antibiotics.
- **Allergic Sinusitis:** Treatment of the nasal allergy with antihistamines also usually relieves the sinus symptoms.

Color of Nasal Discharge With Colds

- The nasal discharge normally changes color during different stages of a cold.
- It starts as a clear discharge and later becomes cloudy.
- Sometimes it becomes yellow or green colored for a few days, and this is still normal.
- Intermittent yellow or green discharge is more common with sleep, antihistamines, or low humidity (Reason: all of these events reduce the production of normal nasal secretions).
- Yellow or green nasal secretions suggest the presence of a bacterial sinusitis ONLY if they occur in combination with sinus pain, OR the return of a fever after it has been gone for more than 24 hours, OR nasal discharge lasts more than 14 days without improvement.
- Nasal secretions need treatment with nasal washes when they block the nose and interfere with breathing through the nose. During a cold, if nasal breathing is noisy but you can't see blockage in the nose, it usually means the dried mucus is farther back. Nasal washes can remove it.

Return to School

- Sinus infections are not contagious. If sinus pain or congestion is associated with a cold or other infection, your child can return to school after the fever is gone and your child feels well enough to participate in normal activities.

See More Appropriate Topic (Instead of This One) If

- Child is younger than 5 years or it doesn't sound like sinus congestion (see Chapter 11, Colds)
- Also has active nasal allergies (see Chapter 12, Hay Fever [Nasal Allergy])

When to Call Your Doctor

Call 911 Now (Your Child May Need an Ambulance) If
- Not moving or too weak to stand

Call Your Doctor Now (Night or Day) If
- Your child looks or acts very sick
- Confused speech or behavior
- Redness or swelling on the cheek or forehead, or around the eye
- Severe pain
- Weak immune system (eg, sickle cell disease, HIV, chemotherapy, organ transplant, chronic steroids)
- Fever above 104°F (40°C) and not improved 2 hours after fever medicine

Call Your Doctor Within 24 Hours (Between 9:00 am and 4:00 pm) If
- You think your child needs to be seen
- Frontal headache present longer than 48 hours
- Fever present more than 3 days
- Fever returns after gone for longer than 24 hours
- Earache occurs
- Sinus pain with fever

Call Your Doctor During Weekday Office Hours If
- You have other questions or concerns
- Sinus pain persists after using nasal washes and pain medicine for 24 hours
- Sinus congestion and fullness lasts more than 2 weeks
- Nasal discharge lasts more than 14 days

Parent Care at Home If
- Sinus congestion as part of a cold and you don't think your child needs to be seen

Home Care Advice for Sinus Congestion

1. **Reassurance**
   - Sinus congestion is a normal part of a cold.
   - Usually, home treatment with nasal washes can prevent an actual bacterial sinus infection.
   - Antibiotics are not helpful for sinus congestion that occurs with colds.

2. **Nasal Washes to Open a Blocked Nose**
   - Use saline nose drops or spray to loosen up the dried mucus. If not available, you can use warm tap water. Teens can just splash warm tap water in the nose and then blow.
   - **Step 1:** Instill 3 drops per nostril.
   - **Step 2:** Blow each nostril separately while closing off the other nostril. Then do other side.
   - **Step 3:** Repeat nose drops and blowing until the discharge is clear.
   - **Frequency:** Do nasal washes whenever your child can't breathe through the nose.
   - Saline nasal sprays can be purchased without a prescription
   - Saline nose drops can also be made—add ½ teaspoon (2 mL) of table salt to 1 cup (8 oz or 240 mL) of warm water.
   - Reason for nose drops: suction or nose blowing alone can't remove dried or sticky mucus.
   - **Another Option:** Use a warm shower to loosen mucus. Breathe in the moist air, then blow each nostril.

3. **Fluids:** Encourage your child to drink adequate fluids to prevent dehydration. This will also thin out nasal secretions and loosen phlegm in the airway.

4. **Humidifier:** If the air in your home is dry, run a humidifier.

5. **Decongestant Nose Spray (No Prescription Needed)**
   - Use this only if sinus still seems blocked up after nasal washes AND your child is 12 years or older. Use the long-acting type (eg, Afrin).
   - **Dosage:** 1 spray on each side 2 times a day.
   - Always clean out the nose before using.
   - Use routinely for 2 days, thereafter only for symptoms.
   - Don't use for more than 5 days (Reason: rebound congestion).

6. **Pain Medicine:** Give acetaminophen (eg, Tylenol) or ibuprofen (eg, Advil) as needed for pain relief (see dosage table in Appendix A or E). The application of a cold pack or ice in a wet washcloth over the sinus for 20 minutes may also help.

7. **Antihistamines:** Give oral antihistamines (eg, Benadryl) only if the child also has nasal allergies (no prescription needed) (see dosage table in Appendix D).

8. **Expected Course**
   - With treatment, viral sinus congestion usually resolves in 7 to 14 days.
   - The main complication occurs if bacteria multiply within the blocked sinus (bacterial sinusitis). This leads to a fever and increased pain. It needs antibiotics.

9. **Contagiousness:** Sinus infections are not contagious. If sinus pain or congestion is associated with a cold or other infection, your child can return to school after the fever is gone and your child feels well enough to participate in normal activities.

10. **Call Your Doctor If**
    - Sinus pain persists for more than 1 day after starting treatment.
    - Sinus congestion persists for more than 2 weeks.
    - Sinus pain present and fever occurs.
    - Your child becomes worse.

And remember, contact your doctor if your child develops any of the "Call Your Doctor" symptoms.

Part 5

Mouth or Throat
Symptoms

Chapter 15

Hand-Foot-and-Mouth Disease

Definition

- A viral infection that causes mouth ulcers and tiny blisters on the hands and feet

Symptoms

- Small, painful ulcers in the mouth, especially on the tongue and sides of the mouth (in all children).
- Small, thick-walled water blisters (like chickenpox) or red spots located on the palms, soles, and webs between the fingers and toes (70%).
- One to 5 water blisters per hand or foot.
- Small blisters or red spots on the buttocks (30%).
- Low-grade fever below 102°F (39°C).
- Mainly occurs in children aged 6 months to 4 years.

Cause

- Coxsackievirus A-16
- Not related to animal disease

Return to School

- Your child can return to child care or school after the fever is gone (usually 2 to 3 days). The rash is not contagious.

See More Appropriate Topic (Instead of This One) If

- Only has mouth ulcers (see Chapter 18, Mouth Ulcers) (EXCEPTION: exposed to hand-foot-and-mouth)
- Only has a rash (see Chapter 43, Rash, Widespread and Cause Unknown)

When to Call Your Doctor

Call Your Doctor Now (Night or Day) If

- Your child looks or acts very sick
- Signs of dehydration (eg, very dry mouth, no tears, no urine in more than 8 hours)
- Stiff neck, severe headache, or acting confused (delirious)

Call Your Doctor Within 24 Hours (Between 9:00 am and 4:00 pm) If

- You think your child needs to be seen
- Red, swollen, and tender gums
- Ulcers and sores also present on outer lip
- Fever present for more than 3 days

Call Your Doctor During Weekday Office Hours If

- You have other questions or concerns

Parent Care at Home If

- Probable hand-foot-and-mouth disease and you don't think your child needs to be seen

Home Care Advice for Hand-Foot-and-Mouth Disease

1. **Reassurance:** Hand-foot-and-mouth disease is a harmless viral rash.
2. **Liquid Antacid for Mouth Pain**
   - Use a liquid antacid 4 times per day.
   - For younger children, put ½ teaspoon (2 mL) in the front of the mouth 4 times per day after meals.
   - Children older than 4 years can use 1 teaspoon (5 mL) as a mouthwash after meals.
3. **Soft Diet**
   - Encourage favorite fluids to prevent dehydration.
   - Cold drinks, milkshakes, popsicles, slushes, and sherbet are good choices.
   - Avoid citrus, salty, or spicy foods.
   - For infants, give fluids by cup, spoon, or syringe rather than a bottle (Reason: the nipple can cause pain).
   - Solid food intake is not important.
4. **Pain or Fever Medicine:** Give acetaminophen (eg, Tylenol) or ibuprofen (eg, Advil) as needed for pain relief or fever above 102°F (39°C) (see dosage table in Appendix A or E).
5. **Contagiousness:** Quite contagious but a mild and harmless disease. Incubation period is 3 to 6 days. Your child can return to child care or school after the fever is gone (usually 2 to 3 days). The rash is not contagious.
6. **Expected Course**
   - The fever lasts 2 or 3 days.
   - Mouth ulcers resolve by 7 days.
   - Rash on the hands and feet lasts 10 days. Rash on the hands and feet may then peel.
7. **Call Your Doctor If**
   - Signs of dehydration develop.
   - Fever present more than 3 days.
   - Your child becomes worse.

> **And remember, contact your doctor if your child develops any of the "Call Your Doctor" symptoms.**

Chapter 16

Lymph Nodes, Swollen

Definition

- Increased size of a lymph node in the neck, armpit, or groin.
- Usually larger than the corresponding node on the other side of the body.
- Normal nodes are usually less than ½ inch (12 mm) across (size of a pea or baked bean).

Causes

- Swollen nodes with a viral infection are usually ½ to 1 inch (12 to 25 mm) across.
- Swollen nodes with a bacterial infection are usually more than 1 inch (25 mm) across (size of a quarter).
- The cervical (neck) nodes are most commonly involved because of the many respiratory infections that occur during childhood.
- Elsewhere, localized nodes are usually reacting to local skin irritation or infection.

Return to School

- Swollen lymph nodes alone are not contagious. If the swollen nodes are associated with a cold, sore throat, or other infection, your child can return to school after the fever is gone and your child feels well enough to participate in normal activities.

See More Appropriate Topic (Instead of This One) If

- Swollen node is in the neck and sore throat is the main symptom (see Chapter 19, Sore Throat)

When to Call Your Doctor

Call Your Doctor Now (Night or Day) If

- Your child looks or acts very sick
- Node in the neck causes difficulty with breathing, swallowing, or drinking
- Fever above 104°F (40°C) and not improved 2 hours after fever medicine
- Overlying skin is red
- Rapid increase in size of node over several hours

Call Your Doctor Within 24 Hours (Between 9:00 am and 4:00 pm) If

- You think your child needs to be seen
- 1 or more inches (2.5 cm or more) in size by measurement
- Very tender to the touch
- Interferes with moving the neck, arm, or leg
- Fever present for more than 3 days

Call Your Doctor During Weekday Office Hours If

- You have other questions or concerns
- In the neck and your child also has a sore throat
- Large nodes at multiple locations
- Cause of the swollen node is unknown
- Child is younger than 1 month
- Large node persists more than 1 month

Parent Care at Home If

- Mildly swollen lymph node and you don't think your child needs to be seen

Home Care Advice for Small Lymph Nodes

1. **Reassurance for Normal Nodes:** If you have discovered a pea- or bean-sized node (smaller than ½ inch or 12 mm), this is a normal lymph node. Don't look for lymph nodes because you can always find some (especially in the neck and groin).

2. **Reassurance for Swollen Nodes From a Viral Infection:** Viral throat infections and colds can cause lymph nodes in the neck to double in size. Slight enlargement and mild tenderness mean the lymph node is fighting the infection and doing a good job.

3. **Pain or Fever Medicine:** Give acetaminophen (eg, Tylenol) or ibuprofen (eg, Advil) as needed for pain relief or fever above 102°F (39°C) (see dosage table in Appendix A or E). Otherwise no treatment is needed.

4. **Avoid Squeezing:** Don't squeeze lymph nodes because it may keep them from shrinking back to normal size. Tell your child not to fidget with them.

5. **Contagiousness:** Swollen lymph nodes alone are not contagious. If the swollen nodes are associated with a cold, sore throat, or other infection, your child can return to school after the fever is gone and your child feels well enough to participate in normal activities.

6. **Expected Course:** After the infection is gone, the nodes slowly return to normal size over 2 to 4 weeks. However, they won't ever completely disappear.

7. **Call Your Doctor If**
   - Node enlarges to more than 1 inch (2.5 cm) in size.
   - Node larger than ½ inch (12 mm) persists more than 1 month.
   - Your child becomes worse.

And remember, contact your doctor if your child develops any of the "Call Your Doctor" symptoms.

Chapter 17

Mouth Injury

Definition

- Injuries to the lip, flap under the upper lip (frenulum), tongue, inner cheeks, floor of the mouth, roof of the mouth (hard and soft palate), or back of the mouth (tonsils and throat)

Types of Mouth Injuries
- Cuts of the **tongue** or inside of the cheeks (from accidentally biting them during eating) are the most common mouth injury. Bites of the tongue rarely need sutures. Even if they gape open a little, if the edges come together when the tongue is quiet, the cut should heal quickly.
- Cuts and bruises of the **upper lip** are usually caused by falls. A tear of the piece of tissue connecting the upper lip to the gum is very common and always heals without sutures. It will re-bleed, however, every time you pull the lip out to look at the bleeding site.
- Cuts of the **lower lip** are usually caused by catching it between the upper and lower teeth during a fall. Most of these cuts do not connect (don't go through the lip). These do not need sutures unless the outer cut is gaping.
- Potentially serious mouth injuries are those to the tonsil, soft palate, or back of the throat (eg, from falling with a pencil or toothbrush in the mouth).

See More Appropriate Topic (Instead of This One) If
- Main injury is to teeth (see Chapter 21, Tooth Injury)

When to Call Your Doctor

Call 911 Now (Your Child May Need an Ambulance) If
- Major bleeding that can't be stopped
- Difficulty breathing

Call Your Doctor Now (Night or Day) If
- You think your child has a serious injury
- Minor bleeding won't stop after 10 minutes of direct pressure
- Gaping cut of tongue or inside the mouth that may need stitches
- Gaping cut through border of lip where it meets the skin
- Severe pain
- Difficulty swallowing fluids or saliva
- Caused by a pencil or other long object and injury to back of mouth
- Mouth looks infected (eg, fever, spreading redness, increasing pain or swelling after 48 hours) (Note: any healing wound in the mouth is normally white for several days.)

Call Your Doctor Within 24 Hours (Between 9:00 am and 4:00 pm) If
- You think your child needs to be seen

Call Your Doctor During Weekday Office Hours If
- You have other questions or concerns

Parent Care at Home If
- Minor mouth injury and you don't think your child needs to be seen

Home Care Advice for Minor Mouth Injuries

1. **Stop Any Bleeding**
   - For bleeding of the inner lip or tissue that connects it to the gum, press the bleeding site against the teeth for 10 minutes.
   - CAUTION: Once bleeding from inside the lip stops, don't pull the lip out again to look at it (Reason: the bleeding will start up again).
   - For bleeding from the tongue, squeeze or press the bleeding site with a sterile gauze or piece of clean cloth for 10 minutes.

2. **Local Cold:** Put a piece of ice or popsicle on the area that was injured for 20 minutes.

3. **Pain Medicine:** If there is pain, give acetaminophen (eg, Tylenol) or ibuprofen (eg, Advil).

4. **Soft Diet**
   - Encourage favorite fluids to prevent dehydration. Cold drinks, milkshakes, and popsicles are especially good.
   - Offer a soft diet. (Avoid foods that need much chewing.)
   - Avoid any salty or citrus foods that might sting.
   - Rinse the wound with warm water immediately after meals.

5. **Expected Course:** Small cuts and scrapes inside the mouth heal up in 3 or 4 days. Infections of mouth injuries are rare.

6. **Call Your Doctor If**
   - Pain becomes severe.
   - Area looks infected (mainly increasing pain or swelling after 48 hours).
   - Fever occurs.
   - Your child becomes worse.

And remember, contact your doctor if your child develops any of the "Call Your Doctor" symptoms.

Chapter 18

Mouth Ulcers

Definition

- Painful, shallow ulcers (sores) on the lining of the mouth.
- The gums and the inner sides of the lips or cheeks are the usual sites.
- Sores on the outer lips (eg, recurrent fever blisters) are excluded.

Causes

- **Canker Sores:** The main cause of 1 or 2 mouth ulcers after 5 years of age. Not contagious.
- **Hand-Foot-and-Mouth Disease:** The most common cause of multiple ulcers in the mouth, mainly on the tongue and sides of the mouth. Caused by coxsackievirus A-16. It is common between ages 1 and 5 years.
- **Herpesvirus (Cold Sore Virus):** The first infection can be severe and cause 10 or more ulcers on the gums, tongue, and lips. Key finding is ulcers on the outer lips or skin around the mouth. Also, fever and difficulty swallowing. Usually occurs at ages 1 to 3 years.

Return to School

- Canker sores are not contagious. Children with fever or many mouth ulcers need to be examined before returning to child care or school.

See More Appropriate Topic (Instead of This One) If

- Have thick-walled, small blisters on the palms or soles, in addition to mouth ulcers (see Chapter 15, Hand-Foot-and-Mouth Disease)

When to Call Your Doctor

Call 911 Now (Your Child May Need an Ambulance) If
- Not moving or too weak to stand

Call Your Doctor Now (Night or Day) If
- Your child looks or acts very sick
- Chemical in mouth could have caused ulcers
- Signs of dehydration (very dry mouth, no tears and no urine in more than 8 hours)

Call Your Doctor Within 24 Hours (Between 9:00 am and 4:00 pm) If
- You think your child needs to be seen
- 4 or more ulcers
- Bloody crusts on lips
- Red, swollen gums
- Ulcers and sores also present on outer lips
- One ulcer on the gum near a tooth with a toothache
- Fever or swollen face
- Large lymph node under the jaw
- Began after starting a medicine

Call Your Doctor During Weekday Office Hours If
- You have other questions or concerns
- Mouth ulcers last more than 2 weeks

Parent Care at Home If
- Probable canker sores and you don't think your child needs to be seen

Home Care Advice for Canker Sores (Harmless Mouth Ulcers)

1. **Canker sores are the number 1 cause of mouth ulcers.**
   - One to 3 painful, white ulcers of the inner cheeks, inner lip, or gums (no fever).
   - Causes include injuries from rough food, toothbrushes, biting, and food irritants.
2. **Liquid Antacid for Pain Relief**
   - Use a liquid antacid 4 times per day for pain relief. (Avoid regular mouthwashes because they sting.)
   - Children older than 4 years can use 1 teaspoon (5 mL) as a mouthwash after meals.
   - For younger children, put ½ teaspoon (2.5 mL) in the front of the mouth after meals.
3. **Pain Medicine:** Give acetaminophen (eg, Tylenol) or ibuprofen (eg, Advil) for severe pain (especially at bedtime).
4. **Fluids**
   - Offer a soft diet.
   - Encourage favorite fluids to prevent dehydration. Cold drinks, milkshakes, and popsicles are especially good.
   - Avoid salty foods, citrus fruits, and foods that need much chewing.
   - For infants, give fluids by cup, spoon, or syringe rather than a bottle (Reason: the nipple can cause pain).
5. **Contagiousness:** Canker sores are not contagious. Children with fever or many mouth ulcers need to be examined before returning to child care or school.
6. **Expected Course:** They heal up in 1 to 2 weeks on their own. Once they occur, no treatment can shorten the course, but treatment can reduce the amount of pain.
7. **Call Your Doctor If**
   - Mouth ulcers last more than 2 weeks.
   - Your child becomes worse.

> **And remember, contact your doctor if your child develops any of the "Call Your Doctor" symptoms.**

Chapter 19

Sore Throat

Definition

- Pain, discomfort, or raw feeling of the throat, especially when swallowing

Causes

- **Colds (Upper Respiratory Infections):** Most sore throats are part of a cold. In fact, a sore throat may be the only symptom for the first 24 hours.
- **Viral Pharyngitis:** Some viruses cause a sore throat without nasal symptoms.
- **Streptococcal Pharyngitis:** Group A streptococcus is the most common bacterial cause. It accounts for 20% of persistent sore throats. Only these need an antibiotic.

Strep Throat

- Symptoms include sore throat, fever, headache, abdominal pain, nausea, and vomiting.
- Cough, hoarseness, red eyes, and runny nose are usually not seen with strep throat and are more suggestive of a viral cause.
- Scarlet fever rash (fine, red, sandpaper-like rash) is highly suggestive of strep throat.
- **Peak Age:** 5 to 15 years old. Uncommon if child is younger than 2 years unless sibling has strep.
- Diagnosis should be confirmed by throat culture prior to starting treatment (there is no risk to your child to delaying treatment until a throat culture can be performed).
- Acute rheumatic fever may occur in children not treated within 10 days of symptom onset.
- Standard treatment is with penicillin or amoxicillin; other antibiotics may sometimes be used.

Symptoms in Infants and Toddlers

- Children younger than 2 years usually don't know how to complain about a sore throat. A young child who refuses previously enjoyed foods or begins to cry during feedings may have a sore throat.

Return to School

- Your child can return to child care or school after the fever is gone and your child feels well enough to participate in normal activities. Children with strep throat also need to be taking an oral antibiotic for 24 hours before they can return.

See More Appropriate Topic (Instead of This One) If

- The main symptom is croup, hoarseness, or cough (see Chapter 24, Croup, or Chapter 23, Cough) (Note: these symptoms are rarely seen with strep.)

When to Call Your Doctor

Call 911 Now (Your Child May Need an Ambulance) If

- Severe difficulty breathing (struggling for each breath, making grunting noises with each breath, unable to speak or cry because of difficulty breathing)

Call Your Doctor Now (Night or Day) If

- Your child looks or acts very sick
- Difficulty breathing, but not severe
- Great difficulty swallowing fluids or saliva
- Stiff neck
- Signs of dehydration (very dry mouth, no tears with crying, and no urine for more than 8 hours)
- Purple or blood-colored spots or dots on skin
- Weak immune system (eg, sickle cell disease, HIV, chemotherapy, organ transplant, chronic steroids)
- Fever above 104°F (40°C) and not improved 2 hours after fever medicine

Call Your Doctor Within 24 Hours (Between 9:00 am and 4:00 pm) If

- You think your child needs an office visit or throat culture
- Sore throat pain is severe and not improved 2 hours after taking ibuprofen (eg, Advil)
- Pink rash that's widespread
- Earache or sinus pain or pressure
- Fever present for more than 3 days
- Fever returns after gone for longer than 24 hours
- Child is younger than 2 years
- Exposure to strep within last 7 days
- Sores present on the skin

Call Your Doctor During Weekday Office Hours If

- Sore throat is the main symptom and persists longer than 48 hours
- Sore throat with cold or cough symptoms is present more than 5 days
- You have other questions or concerns

Parent Care at Home If

- Probable viral throat infection and you don't think your child needs to be seen

Home Care Advice for Sore Throats

1. **Reassurance:** Most sore throats are just part of a cold. The presence of a cough, hoarseness, or nasal discharge points to a cold as the cause of your child's sore throat.

2. **Local Pain Relief**
   - Children older than 1 year can sip warm chicken broth or apple juice.
   - Children older than 6 years can suck on hard candy (eg, butterscotch) or lollipops.
   - Children older than 8 years can also gargle warm water with a little table salt or liquid antacid added.
   - Medicated throat sprays or lozenges are generally not helpful.

3. **Pain or Fever Medicine:** Give acetaminophen (eg, Tylenol) or ibuprofen (eg, Advil) as needed for pain relief or fever above 102°F (39°C) (see dosage table in Appendix A or E).

4. **Soft Diet:** Cold drinks and milkshakes are especially helpful (Reason: swollen tonsils can make some solid foods hard to swallow).

5. **Contagiousness**
   - Your child can return to child care or school after the fever is gone and your child feels well enough to participate in normal activities.
   - Children with strep throat also need to be taking an oral antibiotic for 24 hours before they can return.

6. **Expected Course:** Sore throats with viral illnesses usually last 4 or 5 days.

7. **Call Your Doctor If**
   - Sore throat is the main symptom and lasts longer than 48 hours.
   - Sore throat with a cold lasts more than 5 days.
   - Fever lasts more than 3 days.
   - Your child becomes worse.

> **And remember, contact your doctor if your child develops any of the "Call Your Doctor" symptoms.**

Chapter 20

Strep Throat Exposure

Definition

- Exposure to someone with a strep throat infection.
- Also called close contact.
- Living in the same house as someone (sibling, parent, or other household member) who has a throat culture or rapid strep test that is positive for strep throat.
- Kissing relationship with someone (boyfriend, girlfriend) who has a throat culture or rapid strep test that is positive for strep throat. For this to be relevant, the last close contact to the infected person should be within 10 days of onset of symptoms in exposed child.

Other Types of Contact
- **Limited Contact With Strep:** Exposed to someone outside the home with a positive strep test (eg, at school).
- Sometimes the contact is with a person who was treated for clinical symptoms of a strep infection without any culture or testing.
- If the contact was with someone taking antibiotics for longer than 24 hours, that person is not contagious.
- Throat cultures and rapid strep tests aren't urgent. Most can be done in your doctor's office.

Return to School
- If your child doesn't have any symptoms, he does not need to miss any child care or school.
- If your child has symptoms compatible with strep throat, she should avoid child care or school until results of a throat culture are known.

See More Appropriate Topic (Instead of This One) If
- Sore throat and no known strep throat exposure (see Chapter 19, Sore Throat)
- Sore throat and strep throat exposure more than 10 days ago (see Chapter 19, Sore Throat)

When to Call Your Doctor

Call Your Doctor Now (Night or Day) If

- Your child looks or acts very sick
- Great difficulty swallowing fluids or saliva
- Difficulty breathing or working hard to breathe
- Fever above 104°F (40°C) and not improved 2 hours after fever medicine
- Signs of dehydration (very dry mouth, no tears with crying, and no urine in more than 8 hours)

Call Your Doctor Within 24 Hours (Between 9:00 am and 4:00 pm) If

- You think your child needs an office visit or throat culture
- Sore throat pain is severe and not improved 2 hours after taking ibuprofen (eg, Advil)
- Child is younger than 1 year
- Earache or sinus pain or pressure also present
- Child with mild symptoms compatible with strep throat (eg, sore throat, cries during feedings, puts fingers in mouth, enlarged lymph nodes in neck, fever)

Call Your Doctor During Weekday Office Hours If

- You have other questions or concerns

Parent Care at Home If

- Strep contact but no symptoms and you don't think your child needs to be seen

Home Care Advice for Strep Contacts

Treatment for Contacts WITH Symptoms (Pending a Throat Culture)

1. **Reassurance**
   - A throat culture isn't urgent.
   - It could be strep throat or just a viral infection of the throat.
   - A sore throat is commonly part of a cold.
   - Here are some ways to keep your child comfortable until you get a throat culture.

2. **Local Pain Relief**
   - Children older than 1 year can sip warm chicken broth or apple juice.
   - Children older than 6 years can suck on hard candy (eg, butterscotch) or lollipops.
   - Children older than 8 years can also gargle warm water with a little table salt or liquid antacid added.

3. **Pain or Fever Medicine:** Give acetaminophen (eg, Tylenol) or ibuprofen (eg, Advil) as needed for pain relief or fever above 102°F (39°C) (see dosage table in Appendix A or E).

4. **Soft Diet:** Cold drinks and milkshakes are especially good (Reason: swollen tonsils can make some foods hard to swallow).

5. **Contagiousness:** Your child may have a strep throat infection and should avoid child care or school until the results of the throat culture are known.

6. **Call Your Doctor If**
   - Your child becomes worse.

Treatment for Contacts WITHOUT Symptoms

1. **Reassurance:** Most children exposed to someone with strep throat do not come down with it, especially if exposure occurs outside the home. Throat cultures are unnecessary for children without any symptoms.

2. **Incubation Period:** Most children who do catch strep develop some symptoms 2 to 5 days after exposure.

3. **Contagiousness:** Your child does not need to miss any child care or school.

4. **Call Your Doctor If**
   - Your child develops any strep symptoms in the next 7 days.

> **And remember, contact your doctor if your child develops any of the "Call Your Doctor" symptoms.**

Chapter 21

Tooth Injury

Definition

- Injury to a tooth

Types of Tooth Injuries
- **Loosened Tooth:** May bleed a little from the gums. Usually tightens up on its own.
- Displaced tooth (usually pushed inward).
- Chipped or fractured tooth.
- **Avulsed (Knocked-Out) Tooth:** A dental emergency for permanent teeth.

First Aid Advice for Knocked-Out Permanent Tooth
- To save the tooth, it must be reimplanted as soon as possible (2 hours is the outer limit for survival). Right away is best. If you are more than 30 minutes away from dental or medical care, replace the tooth in the socket before coming in. Use the following technique:
  - Rinse off the tooth with saliva or water (do not scrub it).
  - Replace it in the socket facing the correct way.
  - Press down on the tooth with your thumb until the crown is level with the adjacent tooth.
  - Have your child bite down on a wad of cloth to stabilize the tooth until you can reach your dentist.
- Note: baby teeth can't be reimplanted.

Transporting a Knocked-Out Permanent Tooth
- If unable to put the tooth back in its socket, follow these instructions:
  - It is very important to keep the tooth moist. Do not let it dry out.
  - Transport the tooth in milk or saliva (milk is best per the American Dental Association, 2003).
  - **Milk Transport Option 1 (Best):** Place the tooth in a small plastic bag with some milk. Put the plastic bag in a cup of ice.
  - **Milk Transport Option 2:** Place the tooth in a cup of cold milk.

- **Saliva Transport Option 1:** Put the tooth inside the child's mouth (be careful not to swallow it) (EXCEPTION: Child is younger than 12 years).
- **Saliva Transport Option 2:** Put the tooth in a cup and keep tooth moist with child's saliva (spit).

When to Call Your Doctor

Call Your Dentist or Doctor Now (Night or Day) If

- You think your child has a serious injury
- Permanent tooth knocked out (Reason: needs reimplantation ASAP; 2 hours is the deadline for tooth survival) (See First Aid Advice)
- Permanent tooth is almost falling out
- Baby tooth is almost falling out
- Bleeding won't stop after 10 minutes of direct pressure
- Tooth is greatly pushed out of its normal position
- Tooth that's pushed out of its normal position interferes with normal bite
- Severe pain
- Child is younger than 1 year

Call Your Dentist Within 24 Hours (Between 9:00 am and 4:00 pm) If

- You think your child needs to be seen
- Baby tooth knocked out by injury (Reason: can't be reimplanted but dentist will check for damage to permanent tooth)
- Tooth is slightly pushed out of its normal position
- Can see a chip or fracture line (crack) in the tooth
- Tooth feels very loose when you try to move it

Call Your Dentist During Weekday Office Hours If

- Tooth is sensitive to cold fluids
- Tooth becomes a darker color
- You have other questions or concerns

Parent Care at Home If

- Minor tooth injury and you don't think your child needs to be seen

Home Care Advice for Minor Dental Injuries

1. **Local Cold:** For pain, apply a piece of ice or a popsicle to the injured gum area for 20 minutes.
2. **Pain Medicine:** If it still hurts, give acetaminophen (eg, Tylenol) or ibuprofen (eg, Advil).
3. **Soft Diet:** For any loose teeth, offer a soft diet for 3 days. By then, it should be tightened up.
4. **Call Your Dentist If**
   - Pain becomes severe.
   - Tooth becomes sensitive to hot or cold fluids.
   - Tooth becomes a darker color.
   - Your child becomes worse.

> **And remember, contact your doctor if your child develops any of the "Call Your Doctor" symptoms.**

Part 6

Chest or Breathing
Symptoms

Chapter 22

Asthma Attack

Definition

- Child is having an asthma attack.
- Don't use this chapter unless your child was previously diagnosed as having asthma, asthmatic bronchitis, or reactive airway disease by a physician.

Main Symptom

- A wheeze or whistling (purring) sound on breathing out is the classic symptom.
- Coughing may be the first symptom of an asthma attack.

Causes (Triggers) of Asthma Attacks

- Viral respiratory infections
- Animal contact (especially cats)
- Tobacco smoke or menthol vapors
- Pollens
- Air pollution (eg, barn, circus, wood stove, dirty basement)

Severity of an Asthma Attack

- **Mild:** No shortness of breath (SOB) at rest, mild SOB with walking, speaks normally in sentences, can lay down flat, wheezes only heard by stethoscope (GREEN Zone: peak flow rate 80% to 100% of baseline level or personal best).
- **Moderate:** SOB at rest, speaks in phrases, prefers to sit (can't lay down flat), audible wheezing (YELLOW Zone: peak flow rate 50% to 80% of baseline level).
- **Severe:** Severe SOB at rest, speaks in single words (struggling to breathe), usually loud wheezing or sometimes minimal wheezing because of decreased air movement (RED Zone: peak flow rate less than 50% of baseline level).

When to Call Your Doctor

Call 911 Now (Your Child May Need an Ambulance) If

- Severe difficulty breathing (struggling for each breath, unable to speak or cry because of difficulty breathing, making grunting noises with each breath)
- Your child passed out or has bluish lips or tongue
- Wheezing started suddenly after medicine, an allergic food, or bee sting

Call Your Doctor Now (Night or Day) If

- Your child looks or acts very sick
- Looks like she did when hospitalized before with asthma
- Difficulty breathing not resolved 20 minutes after nebulizer or inhaler
- Peak flow rate lower than 50% of baseline level (personal best) (RED Zone)
- Peak flow rate 50% to 80% of baseline level after using nebulizer or inhaler (YELLOW Zone)
- Wheezing (heard across the room) not resolved 20 minutes after using nebulizer or inhaler
- Continuous (nonstop) coughing that keeps child from playing or sleeping and not improved after using nebulizer or inhaler
- Severe chest pain
- Asthma medicine (nebulizer or inhaler) is needed more frequently than every 4 hours
- Fever above 104°F (40°C) and not improved 2 hours after fever medicine

Call Your Doctor Within 24 Hours (Between 9:00 am and 4:00 pm) If

- You think your child needs to be seen
- Mild wheezing persists longer than 24 hours on treatment
- Sinus pain (not just congestion)
- Fever present for more than 3 days
- Fever returns after gone for longer than 24 hours

Call Your Doctor During Weekday Office Hours If
- You have other questions or concerns
- Don't have written asthma action plan
- Uses an inhaler but doesn't have a spacer
- Missing more than 1 day of school per month for asthma
- Asthma limits exercise or sports
- Asthma attacks frequently awaken child from sleep
- Uses more than 1 inhaler per month
- No asthma checkup in more than 1 year

Parent Care at Home If
- Mild asthma attack and you don't think your child needs to be seen

Home Care Advice for Asthma Attack

1. **Asthma Rescue Medicine**
   - Start your child's quick-relief medicine (eg, albuterol inhaler, nebulizers) at the first sign of any coughing or shortness of breath (don't wait for wheezing) (Reason: early treatment shortens the asthma attack).
   - The best "cough medicine" for a child with asthma is always asthma medicine.
   - Follow your child's action plan for asthma attacks.
   - For albuterol inhalers, give 2 puffs separated by a few minutes, every 4 to 6 hours.
   - Continue the asthma rescue medicine until your child has not wheezed or coughed for 48 hours.
   - **Spacer:** Always use inhalers with a spacer. It will double the amount of medicine that gets to the lungs.
2. **Asthma Controller Medicine:** If your child is using a controller medicine (eg, inhaled steroids, cromolyn), continue to give it as directed.
3. **Hay Fever:** For nose allergy symptoms, it's OK to give antihistamines (Reason: poor control of nasal allergies makes asthma symptoms worse).
4. **Fluids:** Encourage drinking normal amounts of clear fluids (eg, water) (Reason: keeps the lung mucus from becoming sticky).

5. **Humidifier:** If the air is dry, use a humidifier (Reason: to prevent drying of the upper airway).

6. **Avoid or Remove Allergens:** Give a shower to remove pollens, animal dander, or other allergens from the body and hair. Avoid known triggers of asthma attacks (eg, tobacco smoke, feather pillows). Avoid exercise during the attack.

7. **Expected Course:** If treatment is started early, most asthma attacks are quickly brought under control. All wheezing should be gone by 5 days.

8. **Call Your Doctor If**
   - Difficulty breathing occurs.
   - Inhaled asthma medicine (nebulizer or inhaler) is needed more often than every 4 hours.
   - Wheezing persists longer than 24 hours.
   - Your child becomes worse.

And remember, contact your doctor if your child develops any of the "Call Your Doctor" symptoms.

Chapter 23

Cough

Definition

- A cough is the sound made when the cough reflex suddenly forces air and secretions from the lungs.
- A coughing spasm is more than 5 minutes of continuous coughing.

Causes
- Most acute coughs are part of a cold, a viral infection of the large airway (viral bronchitis).
- **Other Common Causes:** Croup, bronchiolitis, asthma, allergic cough, whooping cough.

Sputum or Phlegm
- Yellow or green phlegm is a normal part of the healing process of viral bronchitis.
- This means the lining of the trachea was damaged by the viral infection and is being coughed up as new mucosa replaces it.
- Bacteria do not cause bronchitis in healthy children. Antibiotics are not indicated for the yellow or green phlegm seen with colds.
- The main treatment of a productive cough is to encourage it with good fluid intake, a humidifier (if the air is dry), and warm chicken broth or apple juice for coughing spasms (if child is older than 1 year).

Return to School
- Your child can return to child care or school after the fever is gone and your child feels well enough to participate in normal activities. For practical purposes, the spread of coughs and colds cannot be prevented.

See More Appropriate Topic (Instead of This One) If

- Stridor (harsh sound with breathing in) is present (see Chapter 24, Croup)
- Barky cough and hoarseness (see Chapter 24, Croup)
- Previous diagnosis of asthma (see Chapter 22, Asthma Attack)

When to Call Your Doctor

Call 911 Now (Your Child May Need an Ambulance) If

- Severe difficulty breathing (struggling for each breath, unable to speak or cry because of difficulty breathing, making grunting noises with each breath)
- Child has passed out or stopped breathing
- Lips are bluish when not coughing

Call Your Doctor Now (Night or Day) If

- Your child looks or acts very sick
- Choked on a small object that could be caught in the throat
- Difficulty breathing for child younger than 1 year and not relieved by cleaning the nose
- Difficulty breathing present when not coughing
- Lips have turned bluish during coughing
- Ribs are pulling in with each breath (retractions)
- Can't take a deep breath because of chest pain
- Severe chest pain, coughed up blood, or wheezing
- Weak immune system (eg, sickle cell disease, HIV, chemotherapy, organ transplant, chronic steroids)
- Child is younger than 12 weeks with fever above 100.4°F (38.0°C) rectally (CAUTION: Do NOT give your baby any fever medicine before being seen.)
- Fever above 104°F (40°C) and not improved 2 hours after fever medicine

Call Your Doctor Within 24 Hours (Between 9:00 am and 4:00 pm) If
- You think your child needs to be seen
- Continuous (nonstop) coughing
- Child is younger than 3 months
- Earache or sinus pain (not just congestion) is also present
- Fever present for more than 3 days
- Fever returns after gone for longer than 24 hours
- Chest pain present even when not coughing

Call Your Doctor During Weekday Office Hours If
- You have other questions or concerns
- Coughing has kept child home from school for 3 or more days
- Symptoms of nasal allergy are also present
- Cough has been present more than 3 weeks

Parent Care at Home If
- Cough with no complications and you don't think your child needs to be seen

Home Care Advice for Cough

1. **Reassurance**
   - Coughs are a normal part of a cold.
   - Coughing up mucus is very important for protecting the lungs from pneumonia.
   - We want to encourage a productive cough, not turn it off.

2. **Homemade Cough Medicine**
   - **Goal:** Reduce the irritation or tickle in the throat that triggers a dry cough.
   - **Child Aged 3 Months to 1 Year:** Give warm, clear fluids (eg, warm water, apple juice) to treat the cough. Amount: 1 to 3 teaspoons (5 to 15 mL) 4 times per day when coughing. Avoid honey until 1 year of age.
   - **Child Aged 1 Year and Older:** Use HONEY, ½ to 1 teaspoon (2 to 5 mL), as needed as a homemade cough medicine. It can thin the secretions and loosen the cough. (If not available, you can use corn syrup.)
   - **Child Aged 6 Years and Older:** Use COUGH DROPS to coat the irritated throat. (If not available, you can use hard candy.)

3. **Nonprescription Cough Medicine (Dextromethorphan)**
   - Nonprescription cough medicines are not recommended (Reason: no proven benefit for children and not approved for children younger than 4 years) (Food and Drug Administration, 2008).
   - Honey has been shown to work better for coughs.
   - If you decide to use cough medicine from your drugstore and your child is older than 4 years, choose one with dextromethorphan (DM). It's present in most nonprescription cough syrups.
   - **Indication:** Give only for severe coughs that interfere with sleep, school, or work.
   - **DM Dosage:** See dosage table in Appendix C. Give every 6 to 8 hours for severe coughs that interfere with sleep, school, or work.

4. **Coughing Spasms**
   - Expose to warm mist (eg, foggy bathroom).
   - Give warm fluids to drink (eg, warm water, apple juice) if child is older than 3 months.
   - **Amount:** If child is 3 months to 1 year of age, give warm fluids in a dosage of 1 to 3 teaspoons (5 to 15 mL) 4 times per day when coughing. If child is older than 1 year, use unlimited amounts as needed.
   - Reason: relax the airway and loosen up the phlegm.
5. **Vomiting:** For vomiting that occurs with hard coughing, reduce the amount given per feeding (eg, in infants, give 2 oz less formula) (Reason: cough-induced vomiting is more common with a full stomach).
6. **Fluids:** Encourage your child to drink adequate fluids to prevent dehydration. This will also thin out nasal secretions and loosen phlegm in the airway.
7. **Humidifier:** If the air is dry, use a humidifier (Reason: dry air makes coughs worse).
8. **Fever Medicine:** For fever above 102°F (39°C), give acetaminophen (eg, Tylenol) or ibuprofen (eg, Advil) (see dosage table in Appendix A or E).
9. **Avoid Tobacco Smoke:** Active or passive smoking makes coughs much worse.
10. **Contagiousness:** Your child can return to child care or school after the fever is gone and your child feels well enough to participate in normal activities. For practical purposes, the spread of coughs and colds cannot be prevented.
11. **Extra Advice: Antihistamines for Allergic Cough**
    - Antihistamines can bring an allergic cough and nasal allergy symptoms under control within 1 hour.
    - Benadryl or chlorpheniramine (CTM) products are very effective and no prescription is needed.
    - They need to be given every 6 to 8 hours (see dosage table in Appendix B or D).

12. **Expected Course**
- Viral bronchitis causes a cough for 2 to 3 weeks.
- Sometimes your child will cough up lots of phlegm (mucus). The mucus can normally be gray, yellow, or green.
- Antibiotics are not helpful.

13. **Call Your Doctor If**
- Difficulty breathing occurs.
- Wheezing occurs.
- Cough lasts more than 3 weeks.
- Your child becomes worse.

> **And remember, contact your doctor if your child develops any of the "Call Your Doctor" symptoms.**

Chapter 24

Croup

Definition

- Viral infection of the voice box (larynx).
- Croupy cough is tight, low pitched, and barky (like a barking seal).
- The voice or cry is hoarse (laryngitis).

Stridor: A Complication of Croup
- Stridor is a harsh, raspy sound heard with breathing in.
- Loud or continuous stridor means severe croup.
- All stridor needs to be treated with warm mist.
- See First Aid Advice for treatment recommendations.

Cause
- Usually a parainfluenza virus

Return to School
- Your child can return to child care or school after the fever is gone and your child feels well enough to participate in normal activities. For practical purposes, the spread of croup and colds cannot be prevented.

See More Appropriate Topic (Instead of This One) If
- It doesn't sound like croup (see Chapter 23, Cough)

First Aid Advice for Stridor (Harsh Sound With Breathing in) or Constant Coughing
- Breathe warm mist in a foggy bathroom with the hot shower running for 20 minutes. Other options: a wet washcloth held near the face or a humidifier containing warm water.
- CAUTION: Avoid very hot water or steam, which could cause burns or high body temperatures.
- If warm mist fails, breathe cool air by standing near an open refrigerator or taking your child outside for a few minutes if the weather is cold.

When to Call Your Doctor

Call 911 Now (Your Child May Need an Ambulance) If

- Severe difficulty breathing (struggling for each breath, unable to speak or cry because of difficulty breathing, continuous severe stridor)
- Child has passed out or stopped breathing
- Lips are bluish when not coughing
- Croup started suddenly after bee sting, taking a medicine, or allergic food
- Child is drooling, spitting, or having great difficulty swallowing (EXCEPTION: drooling due to teething)

Call Your Doctor Now (night or day) If

- Note: for any stridor, difficulty breathing, or severe coughing, see First Aid Advice
- Stridor (harsh noise with breathing in) is present now
- Your child looks or acts very sick
- Child choked on a small object that could be caught in the throat
- Difficulty breathing (child younger than 1 year) not relieved by cleaning the nose
- Difficulty breathing (child older than 1 year) present when not coughing
- Lips have turned bluish during coughing
- Ribs are pulling in with each breath (retractions)
- Child can't bend the neck forward
- Severe chest pain
- Child is younger than 6 months with any stridor
- Weak immune system (eg, sickle cell disease, HIV, chemotherapy, organ transplant, chronic steroids)
- Fever above 104°F (40°C) and not improved 2 hours after fever medicine
- Child is younger than 12 weeks with fever above 100.4°F (38.0°C) rectally (CAUTION: Do NOT give your baby any fever medicine before being seen.)

Call Your Doctor Within 24 Hours (Between 9:00 am and 4:00 pm) If

- You think your child needs to be seen
- Had croup before that needed Decadron
- Stridor (harsh noise with breathing in) occurred but not present now
- Continuous (nonstop) coughing
- Child is younger than 3 months with a croupy cough
- Earache is also present
- Fever present for more than 3 days
- Fever returns after gone for longer than 24 hours

Call Your Doctor During Weekday Office Hours If

- You have other questions or concerns
- Croup is a recurrent problem (has occurred 3 or more times)
- Barky cough present more than 14 days

Parent Care at Home If

- Mild croup with no complications and you don't think your child needs to be seen

Home Care Advice for Croupy Cough

1. **Reassurance**
   - Most children with croup just have a barky cough.
   - Some develop tight breathing (called stridor).
   - Remember that coughing up mucus is very important for protecting the lungs from pneumonia.
   - We want to encourage a productive cough, not turn it off.

2. **Humidifier:** If the air is dry, run a humidifier in the bedroom (Reason: dry air makes croup worse).

3. **Homemade Cough Medicine**
   - **Goal:** Reduce the irritation or tickle in the throat that triggers a dry cough.
   - **Child Aged 3 Months to 1 Year:** Give warm, clear fluids (eg, warm water, apple juice) to treat the cough. Amount: 1 to 3 teaspoons (5 to 15 mL) 4 times per day when coughing. Avoid honey until 1 year of age.
   - **Child Aged 1 Year and Older:** Use HONEY, ½ to 1 teaspoon (2 to 5 mL), as needed as a homemade cough medicine. It can thin the secretions and loosen the cough. (If not available, you can use corn syrup.)
   - **Child Aged 6 Years and Older:** Use COUGH DROPS to coat the irritated throat. (If not available, you can use hard candy.)

4. **Nonprescription Cough Medicine (Dextromethorphan)**
   - Nonprescription cough medicines are not recommended (Reason: no proven benefit for children). Never use them if younger than 4 years (Reason: risk of serious side effects and not approved by Food and Drug Administration).
   - Honey has been shown to work better for coughs.
   - If you decide to use cough medicine from your drugstore and your child is older than 4 years, choose one with dextromethorphan (DM). It's present in most nonprescription cough syrups.
   - **Indication:** Give only for severe coughs that interfere with sleep, school, or work.
   - **DM Dosage:** See dosage table in Appendix C. Give every 6 to 8 hours for severe coughs that interfere with sleep, school, or work.

5. **Coughing Spasms**
   - Expose to warm mist (eg, foggy bathroom).
   - Give warm fluids to drink (eg, warm water, apple juice) if older than 3 months.
   - **Amount:** If child is 3 months to 1 year of age, give warm fluids in a dosage of 1 to 3 teaspoons (5 to 15 mL) 4 times per day when coughing. If child is older than 1 year, use unlimited amounts as needed.
   - Reason: relax the airway and loosen up the phlegm.
6. **Fluids:** Encourage your child to drink adequate fluids to prevent dehydration. This will also thin out nasal secretions and loosen phlegm in the airway.
7. **Fever Medicine:** For fever above 102°F (39°C), give acetaminophen (eg, Tylenol) or ibuprofen (eg, Advil) (see dosage table in Appendix A or E).
8. **Observation During Sleep:** Sleep in the same room with your child for a few nights (Reason: can suddenly develop stridor at night).
9. **Avoid Tobacco Smoke:** Active or passive smoking makes coughs much worse.
10. **Contagiousness:** Your child can return to child care or school after the fever is gone and your child feels well enough to participate in normal activities. For practical purposes, the spread of croup and colds cannot be prevented.
11. **Expected Course:** Croup usually lasts 5 to 6 days and becomes worse at night.
12. **Call Your Doctor If**
    - Stridor (harsh raspy sound) occurs.
    - Croupy cough lasts more than 14 days.
    - Your child becomes worse.

> **And remember, contact your doctor if your child develops any of the "Call Your Doctor" symptoms.**

Chapter 25

Influenza, Seasonal

Definition

- Influenza (flu) is a viral infection of the nose, throat, trachea, and bronchi.
- You think your child has influenza because other family members have it.
- You think your child has regular (seasonal) influenza and it's prevalent in the community.

Symptoms

- Main symptoms are a runny nose, sore throat, bad cough, and fever. If there is no fever, your child probably doesn't have flu.
- More muscle pain, headache, fever, and chills than with usual colds.

Cause

- Influenza viruses that change yearly

Prevention With Influenza Vaccine (Flu Shot)

- Yearly flu shots prevent 70% to 90% of influenza.
- They are recommended for all children older than 6 months.
- New flu vaccine is usually available every year by October.

Diagnosis: How to Know Your Child Has Influenza

- If influenza is widespread in your community and your child has flu symptoms with fever, she probably has the flu. You don't need to get any special tests. You should call your doctor if your child is HIGH RISK for complications of the flu (see the list on page 126). For LOW-RISK children, you don't need to call or see your child's doctor unless your child develops a possible complication of the flu (see "When to Call Your Doctor").

HIGH-RISK Children for Complications From Influenza

- Children are considered HIGH RISK for complications if they have any of the following conditions:
  - Lung disease (eg, asthma).
  - Heart disease (eg, congenital heart disease).
  - Cancer or weak immune system conditions.
  - Neuromuscular disease (eg, muscular dystrophy).
  - Diabetes, sickle cell disease, kidney disease, or liver disease.
  - Diseases requiring long-term aspirin therapy.
  - Pregnancy.
  - Healthy children younger than 2 years are also considered HIGH RISK (Centers for Disease Control and Prevention [CDC], September 2009).
  - Note: all other children are referred to as LOW RISK.

Prescription Antiviral Drugs for Influenza

- Antiviral drugs (eg, Tamiflu) must be started within 48 hours of the start of flu symptoms to have an effect.
- The CDC recommends they be used for any patient with severe symptoms AND for all HIGH-RISK children (see the previous list).
- The CDC doesn't recommend antiviral drugs for LOW-RISK children with mild flu symptoms.
- Their benefits are limited—they usually reduce the time your child is sick by 1 to 1½ days. They reduce the symptoms but do not cure the disease.
- **Side Effects:** Vomiting in 10% of children.

Return to School

- Your child can return to child care or school after the fever is gone for 24 hours and your child feels well enough to participate in normal activities.
- Spread is rapid because the incubation period is only 2 days (range: 1 to 4 days) and the virus is very contagious.

See More Appropriate Topic (Instead of This One) If

- Influenza vaccine reaction suspected (see Chapter 38, Immunization Reactions)

When to Call Your Doctor

Call 911 Now (Your Child May Need an Ambulance) If

- Severe difficulty breathing (struggling for each breath, making grunting noises with each breath, unable to speak or cry because of difficulty breathing)
- Lips or face are bluish when not coughing

Call Your Doctor Now (Night or Day) If

- Your child looks or acts very sick
- Difficulty breathing (younger than 1 year) not relieved by cleaning the nose
- Difficulty breathing (older than 1 year) present when not coughing
- Breathing becomes very rapid
- Lips or face have turned bluish during coughing
- Wheezing (tight, purring sound with breathing out)
- Stridor (harsh sound with breathing in)
- Ribs are pulling in with each breath (retractions)
- Chest pain and can't take a deep breath
- Dehydration suspected (no urine for more than 8 hours AND very dry mouth, no tears, ill-appearing)
- Weak immune system (eg, sickle cell disease, HIV, chemotherapy, organ transplant, chronic steroids)
- **SEVERE HIGH-RISK Patient:** Chronic lung disease (EXCEPTION: mild asthma), heart disease, bedridden
- Child is younger than 12 weeks with fever above 100.4°F (38.0°C) rectally (CAUTION: Do NOT give your baby any fever medicine before being seen.)
- Fever above 104°F (40°C) and not improved 2 hours after fever medicine

Call Your Doctor Within 24 Hours (Between 9:00 am and 4:00 pm) If
- You think your child needs to be seen
- HIGH RISK for complications of flu (children with other chronic diseases [see list on page 126] OR healthy younger than 2 years)
- Continuous (nonstop) coughing
- Child is younger than 3 months with any cough
- Earache or ear discharge also present
- Sinus pain (not just congestion) is also present
- Fever present for more than 3 days
- Fever returns after gone for longer than 24 hours

Call Your Doctor During Weekday Office Hours If
- You have other questions or concerns
- Child is older than 6 months and needs flu shot
- Coughing has kept home from school for 3 or more days
- Nasal discharge lasts more than 2 weeks
- Cough lasts more than 3 weeks
- Flu symptoms last more than 3 weeks

Parent Care at Home If
- Probable seasonal influenza with no complications, your child is LOW RISK, and you don't think your child needs to be seen

Home Care Advice for Seasonal Influenza

1. **Reassurance**
   - Because influenza is widespread in your community and your child has flu symptoms (cough, sore throat, runny nose, and fever), your child probably has the flu.
   - Special tests are not needed.
   - You don't need to call or see your child's doctor unless your child develops a possible complication of the flu (eg, earache, difficulty breathing).
   - For healthy people, the symptoms of seasonal influenza are similar to those of the common cold.
   - With flu, however, the onset is more abrupt and symptoms are more severe. Feeling very sick for the first 3 days is common.
   - The treatment of influenza depends on your child's main symptoms and is usually no different from that used for other viral respiratory infections.
   - Bed rest is unnecessary.

2. **Runny Nose With Profuse Discharge: Blow or Suction the Nose**
   - Nasal mucus is washing viruses and bacteria out of the nose and sinuses. Blowing the nose is all that's needed. For younger children, gently suction the nose with a suction bulb.
   - Apply petroleum jelly to the nasal openings to protect them from irritation.
   - Cleanse the skin first.

3. **Nasal Washes to Open a Blocked Nose**
   - Use saline nose drops or spray to loosen up the dried mucus. If not available, you can use warm tap water.
   - **Step 1:** Instill 3 drops per nostril. (If child is younger than 1 year, use 1 drop and do 1 side at a time.)
   - **Step 2:** Blow (or suction) each nostril separately, while closing off the other nostril. Then do other side.
   - **Step 3:** Repeat nose drops and blowing (or suctioning) until the discharge is clear.
   - **Frequency:** Do nasal washes whenever your child can't breathe through the nose.
   - Saline nasal sprays can be purchased without a prescription.

- Saline nose drops can also be made—add ½ teaspoon (2 mL) of table salt to 1 cup (8 oz or 240 mL) of warm water.
- Reason for nose drops: suction or nose blowing alone can't remove dried or sticky mucus.
- **Another Option:** Use a warm shower to loosen mucus. Breathe in the moist air, then blow each nostril.
- For young children, you can also use a wet cotton swab to remove sticky mucus.
- **Importance for a Young Infant:** Can't nurse or drink from a bottle unless the nose is open.

4. **Medicines for Colds**
   - **Cold medicines** are not recommended at any age. (Reason: they are not helpful. They can't remove dried mucus from the nose. Nasal washes can.)
   - **Antihistamines** are not helpful, unless your child also has nasal allergies.
   - **Decongestants:** Over-the-counter oral decongestants (pseudo-ephedrine or phenylephrine) are not recommended. Although they may reduce nasal congestion in some children, they also can have side effects.
   - **Age Limit:** Before 4 years of age, never use any cough or cold medicines (Reason: unsafe and not approved by Food and Drug Administration). (Avoid multi-ingredient products at any age.)
   - **No Antibiotics:** Antibiotics are not helpful, unless your child develops an ear or sinus infection.

5. **Homemade Cough Medicine**
   - **Goal:** Reduce the irritation or tickle in the throat that triggers a dry cough.
   - **Child Aged 3 Months to 1 Year:** Give warm, clear fluids (eg, warm water, apple juice) to treat the cough. Dosage: 1 to 3 teaspoons (5 to 15 mL) 4 times per day when coughing. Avoid honey until 1 year of age.
   - **Child Aged 1 Year and Older:** Use HONEY, ½ to 1 teaspoon (2 to 5 mL), as needed as a homemade cough medicine. It can thin the secretions and loosen the cough. (If not available, you can use corn syrup.) Drugstore cough medicines are not as helpful as honey.

- **Child Aged 6 Years and Older:** Use COUGH DROPS to coat the irritated throat. (If not available, you can use hard candy.)
6. **Sore Throat Relief:** For mild sore throat, use warm chicken broth for child older than 1 year and hard candy for child older than 6 years. For throat pain more than mild, ibuprofen (eg, Advil) is very effective (see dosage table in Appendix E).
7. **Fluids:** Encourage adequate fluids to prevent dehydration.
8. **Fever Medicine**
   - For fever above 102°F (39°C) or discomfort, use acetaminophen (eg, Tylenol) or ibuprofen (eg, Advil) (see dosage table in Appendix A or E).
   - **Avoid aspirin** because of the strong link with Reye syndrome.
   - **For All Fevers:** Give cold fluids in unlimited amounts. Avoid excessive clothing or blankets (bundling).
9. **Pain Medicine:** For pain relief (eg, muscle aches, headaches), give acetaminophen (eg, Tylenol) every 4 hours OR ibuprofen (eg, Advil) every 6 hours as needed (see dosage table in Appendix A or E).
10. **Prescription Antiviral Drugs for Influenza**
    - Antiviral drugs (eg, Tamiflu) must be started within 48 hours of the start of flu symptoms to have an effect.
    - The CDC recommends they be used for any patient with severe symptoms AND for all HIGH-RISK children (see list on page 126).
    - The CDC doesn't recommend antiviral drugs for LOW-RISK children with mild flu symptoms.
    - Their benefits are limited—they usually reduce the time your child is sick by 1 to 1½ days. They reduce the symptoms but do not eliminate them.
    - **Side Effects:** Vomiting in 10% of children.
11. **Contagiousness**
    - Spread is rapid because the incubation period is only 2 days and the virus is very contagious.
    - Your child can return to child care or school after the fever is gone for 24 hours and your child feels well enough to participate in normal activities.

12. **Expected Course**
    - Influenza causes a cough that lasts 2 to 3 weeks.
    - Sometimes your child will cough up lots of phlegm (mucus). The mucus can normally be gray, yellow, or green.
    - Coughing up mucus is very important for protecting the lungs from pneumonia.
    - We want to encourage a productive cough, not turn it off.
    - Fever lasts 2 to 3 days and runny nose lasts 7 to 14 days.
13. **Prevention: How to Protect Yourself From Getting Sick**
    - Wash hands often with soap and water.
    - Alcohol-based hand cleaners are also effective.
    - Avoid touching the eyes, nose, or mouth. Germs on the hands can spread this way.
    - Try to avoid close contact with sick people.
    - Try to avoid unnecessary visits to the emergency department and urgent care centers because those are places where you are more likely to be exposed to flu, if you don't have it.
14. **Prevention: How to Protect Others—Stay Home When Sick**
    - Cover the nose and mouth with a tissue when coughing or sneezing.
    - Wash hands often with soap and water, especially after coughing or sneezing.
    - Limit contact with others to keep from infecting them.
    - Stay home from school or work for at least 24 hours after the fever is gone (CDC, August 2009).
15. **Call Your Doctor If**
    - Breathing becomes difficult or rapid.
    - Retractions (pulling in between the ribs) occur.
    - Dehydration occurs.
    - Earache or sinus pain occurs.
    - Fever lasts more than 3 days.
    - Nasal discharge lasts more than 14 days.
    - Cough lasts more than 3 weeks.
    - Your child becomes worse.

And remember, contact your doctor if your child develops any of the "Call Your Doctor" symptoms.

Part 7

Abdomen
Symptoms

Chapter 26

Abdominal Pain

Definition

- Pain or discomfort located between the bottom of the rib cage and the groin crease.
- The older child complains of a stomachache.
- The younger child should at least point to or hold the abdomen.

Causes

- **Indigestion:** Indigestion or overeating causes many mild stomachaches.
- **Gastroenteritis:** A viral infection of the intestines causes stomach cramps as well as vomiting or diarrhea.
- **Food Poisoning:** Severe vomiting or diarrhea lasting fewer than 12 hours is often caused by bacterial overgrowth in unrefrigerated foods.
- **Constipation:** The need to pass a stool causes lower abdominal cramps.
- **Strep:** Strep throat causes up to 10% of acute abdominal pain.
- **Serious Causes:** These include appendicitis, kidney infections, and intussusception. Suspect appendicitis if pain is low on the right side, the child walks bent over, the child won't hop or jump, and the child prefers to lie still.
- **Stress:** The most common cause of recurrent stomachaches is stress (commonly called the "worried stomach"). More than 10% of children have them. These children tend to be sensitive, serious, conscientious, even model children. This can make them more vulnerable to the normal stresses of life, such as changing schools, moving, or family disagreements. The pain occurs in the pit of the stomach or near the belly button. The pain is mild but real.

See More Appropriate Topic (Instead of This One) If

- Constipation present and is the main symptom (see Chapter 27, Constipation)
- Diarrhea present and is the main symptom (see Chapter 28, Diarrhea)
- Urination pain present and abdominal pain is mild (see Chapter 31, Urination Pain)
- Vomiting (or child feels need to vomit) is the main symptom (see Chapter 30, Vomiting Without Diarrhea)
- Crying and not sure what's causing it (see Chapter 1, Crying)

When to Call Your Doctor

Call 911 Now (Your Child May Need an Ambulance) If

- Not moving or too weak to stand

Call Your Doctor Now (Night or Day) If

- Your child looks or acts very sick
- You suspect poisoning with a plant, medicine, or chemical
- Unable to walk or walks bent over holding the abdomen
- Pain mainly low on the right side
- Pain or swelling in the scrotum or testicle (male)
- Could be pregnant (female)
- Severe pain anywhere
- Constant pain (or crying) present longer than 2 hours
- Blood in the stool or vomiting blood
- Vomiting bile (bright yellow or green)
- Recent injury to the abdomen
- Child is younger than 2 years
- Fever above 104°F (40°C) and not improved 2 hours after fever medicine

Call Your Doctor Within 24 Hours (Between 9:00 am and 4:00 pm) If

- You think your child needs to be seen
- Mild pain that comes and goes (cramps) lasts longer than 24 hours
- Fever is present

Call Your Doctor During Weekday Office Hours If
- You have other questions or concerns
- Abdominal pains are a recurrent chronic problem

Parent Care at Home If
- Mild abdominal pain and you don't think your child needs to be seen

Home Care Advice for Mild Abdominal Pain

1. **Reassurance**
   - A mild stomachache can be caused by something as simple as gas pains or overeating.
   - Sometimes a stomachache signals the onset of a vomiting or diarrhea illness from a virus (gastroenteritis). Watching your child for 2 hours will usually tell you the cause.
2. **Rest:** Encourage your child to lie down and rest until feeling better.
3. **Clear Fluids:** Offer clear fluids only (eg, water, flat soft drinks, half-strength Gatorade). For mild pain, offer a regular diet.
4. **Prepare for Vomiting:** Keep a vomiting pan handy. Younger children often refer to nausea as a stomachache.
5. **Pass a Stool:** Encourage sitting on the toilet and trying to pass a stool. This may relieve pain if it is caused by constipation or impending diarrhea. (Note: for constipation, sitting in warm water may relax the anus and help release a stool.)
6. **Avoid Medicines:** Any drug (especially ibuprofen [eg, Advil]) could irritate the stomach lining and make the pain worse. Do not give any pain medicines or laxatives for stomach cramps. For fever above 102°F (39°C), acetaminophen (eg, Tylenol) can be given.
7. **Expected Course:** With harmless causes, the pain is usually better or resolved in 2 hours. With gastroenteritis (stomach flu), belly cramps may precede each bout of vomiting or diarrhea and last several days. With serious causes (eg, appendicitis), the pain worsens and becomes constant.

8. **Call Your Doctor If**
   - Pain becomes severe.
   - Constant pain present longer than 2 hours.
   - Mild pain that comes and goes present longer then 24 hours.
   - Your child becomes worse.
9. **Worried Stomach: Extra Advice**
   - Help your child talk about events that trigger abdominal pain and how to cope with these triggers next time.
   - Help your child worry less about things he can't control.
   - Teach your child to use relaxation exercises (relaxing every muscle in the body) to treat the pain. Lie down in a quiet place; take deep, slow breaths; and think about something pleasant. Listening to CDs or audiotapes that teach relaxation might help.
   - Teach your child the importance of getting adequate sleep.
   - Make sure that your child doesn't miss any school because of stomachaches. Stressed children have a tendency to want to stay home when the going gets rough.
   - CAUTION: Your child should have a complete medical checkup before you conclude that recurrent stomachaches are caused by worrying too much.

> **And remember, contact your doctor if your child develops any of the "Call Your Doctor" symptoms.**

Chapter 27

Constipation

Definition

- Pain or crying during the passage of a stool (bowel movement) OR
- Unable to pass a stool after straining or pushing longer than 10 minutes OR
- Three or more days without a stool (EXCEPTION: breastfed and older than 1 month)

Imitators of Constipation
- **If Breastfed and Older Than 1 Month:** Infrequent stools every 4 to 7 days that are soft, large, and pain free can be normal. Before 1 month of age, infrequent stools usually mean an inadequate intake of breast milk.
- Grunting or straining while pushing out a stool is normal in young infants (Reason: difficult to pass stool lying on back with no help from gravity). Infants commonly become red in the face during straining.
- Brief straining or pushing for less than 10 minutes can occur occasionally at any age.
- **Large Stools:** Size relates to amount of food consumed and stool frequency. Large eaters have larger stools.
- Hard or dry stools are also normal if passed easily without straining. Often relates to poor fiber intake. Some children even have small, dry, rabbit-pellet–like stools.

Causes
- High milk or cheese diet
- Low fiber diet
- Postponing stools
- Slow intestinal transit time (genetic differences)

See More Appropriate Topic (Instead of This One) If

- Doesn't meet the definition of constipation (see Chapter 26, Abdominal Pain)

When to Call Your Doctor

Call Your Doctor Now (Night or Day) If

- Your child looks or acts very sick
- Persistent abdominal pain longer than 1 hour (includes persistent crying)
- Persistent rectal pain longer than 1 hour (includes persistent straining)
- Vomiting more than 3 times in last 2 hours
- Child is younger than 1 month and breastfed
- Child is younger than 12 months with recent onset of weak cry, weak suck, or weak muscles

Call Your Doctor Within 24 Hours (Between 9:00 am and 4:00 pm) If

- You think your child needs to be seen
- Child is younger than 2 months (EXCEPTION: normal straining and grunting)
- Bleeding from anal fissures (tears)
- Needs to pass stool BUT afraid to release OR refuses to go
- Child may be "blocked up"

Call Your Doctor During Weekday Office Hours If

- You have other questions or concerns
- Leaking stool
- Suppository or enema needed recently to relieve pain
- Infrequent stools continue after dietary changes (EXCEPTION: normal if breastfed infant older than 1 month AND stools are not painful)
- Toilet training is in progress
- Painful stools occur 3 or more times
- Constipation is a recurrent chronic problem

Parent Care at Home If

- Mild constipation and you don't think your child needs to be seen

Home Care Advice for Constipation

1. **Normal Stools**
   - Once children are on a regular diet (age 1 year), the normal range for stools is 3 per day to 1 every 2 days.
   - The "every 4- and 5-day" kids all have pain with passage and prolonged straining.
   - The "every 3-day" kids usually drift into longer intervals and then develop symptoms.
   - Passing a stool should be fun, or at least free of discomfort.
   - Any child with discomfort during stool passage or prolonged straining at least needs treatment with dietary changes.

2. **Diet for Infants Younger Than 1 Year**
   - For infants older than 1 month only on breast milk or formula, add fruit juices, 1 oz (30 mL) per month of age per day. Pear or apple juice is OK at any age (Reason: treating a symptom).
   - For infants older than 4 months, also add baby foods with high fiber content twice a day (peas, beans, apricots, prunes, peaches, pears, plums).
   - If on finger foods, add cereal and small pieces of fresh fruit.

3. **Diet for Children Older Than 1 Year**
   - Increase fruit juice (apple, pear, cherry, grape, prune) (Note: citrus fruit juices are not helpful).
   - Add fruits and vegetables high in fiber content (peas, beans, broccoli, bananas, apricots, peaches, pears, figs, prunes, dates) 3 or more times per day.
   - Increase whole grain foods (bran flakes, bran muffins, graham crackers, oatmeal, brown rice, whole wheat bread; popcorn can be used if older than 4 years).
   - Limit milk products (milk, ice cream, cheese, yogurt) to 3 servings per day.

4. **Stop Toilet Training:** Temporarily put your child back in diapers or pull-ups.
   - Reassure her that the poops won't hurt when they come out.
   - Praise her for the release of stools.
   - Avoid any pressure, punishment, or power struggles about holding back poops, sitting on the potty, or resistance to training.

5. **Sitting on the Toilet (if Toilet Trained):** Establish a regular bowel pattern by sitting on the toilet for 10 minutes after meals, especially breakfast.

6. **Warm Water for Rectal Pain:** Warmth helps many children relax the anal sphincter and release a stool. For prolonged straining, have your child sit in warm water or apply a warm, wet cotton ball to the anus.

7. **Flexed Position**
   - Help your baby by holding the knees against the chest to simulate squatting (the natural position for pushing out a stool). It's difficult to have a stool while lying down.
   - Gently pumping the lower abdomen may also help.

8. **Call Your Doctor If**
   - Constipation continues after making dietary changes.
   - Your child becomes worse.

And remember, contact your doctor if your child develops any of the "Call Your Doctor" symptoms.

Chapter 28

Diarrhea

Definition

- Diarrhea is the sudden increase in the frequency and looseness of stools.
- The main risk of diarrhea is dehydration.
- Loose or runny stools do not cause dehydration.
- Frequent, watery stools can cause dehydration.

Causes

- **Viral gastroenteritis** (viral infection of the stomach and intestines) is the usual cause.
- **Bacteria** (eg, *Salmonella, Shigella)* cause some diarrhea. The main food-borne bacteria are *Campylobacter, Salmonella,* and *Escherichia coli.*
- **Food Poisoning:** Rapid onset of vomiting and diarrhea within hours after eating a food contaminated with toxins (eg, cream dishes that are not properly refrigerated). Symptoms usually resolve in fewer than 24 hours without a need for medical care.
- *Giardia* (a parasite) occasionally, especially in child care centers.

How to Recognize Dehydration

- Dehydration means that the body has lost excessive fluids, usually from vomiting or diarrhea. An associated weight loss of more than 3% is required. In general, mild diarrhea, mild vomiting, or a mild decrease in fluid intake does not cause dehydration.
- Dehydration is the most important complication of diarrhea.
- The following are signs of dehydration:
  - Decreased urination (no urine in more than 8 hours) occurs early in the process of dehydration. So does a dark-yellow, concentrated yellow. If the urine is light straw colored, your child is not dehydrated.
  - Dry tongue and inside of the mouth. Dry lips are not helpful.
  - Dry eyes with decreased or absent tears.

- In infants, a depressed or sunken soft spot.
- Delayed capillary refill longer than 2 seconds. This refers to the return of a pink color to the thumbnail after you press it and make it pale. Ask your child's doctor to teach you how to do this test.
- Irritable, tired out, or acting ill. If your child is alert, happy, and playful, he is not dehydrated.
- A child with severe dehydration becomes too weak to stand or very dizzy if he tries to stand.

Definition of Diarrhea in Breastfed Infants

- The stools of a breastfed infant are normal unless they contain mucus or blood, or develop a new bad odor.
- The looseness (normally runny and seedy), color (normally yellow), and frequency of stools (normally more than 6 a day) are not much help. Breastfed babies may normally even pass some green stools surrounded by a water ring (normal bile can come out green if intestinal transit time is rapid enough).
- During the first 1 to 2 months of life, the breastfed baby may normally pass a stool after each feeding. (However, if an infant's stools abruptly increase in number and looseness and persist for 3 or more stools, the baby probably has diarrhea.)
- Other clues to diarrhea are poor eating, acting sick, or fever.

Definition of Diarrhea in Formula-Fed Infants

- Formula-fed babies pass 1 to 8 stools per day during the first week, then 1 to 4 per day until 2 months of age.
- The stools are yellow in color and peanut butter in consistency.
- Formula-fed newborns have true diarrhea if the stools abruptly increase in number or looseness and persist for 3 or more stools, become watery or very runny, contain mucus or blood, or develop a new bad odor.
- Other clues to diarrhea are poor eating, acting sick, or fever.
- After 2 months of age, most infants pass 1 or 2 stools per day (or 1 every other day) and no longer appear to have mild diarrhea.

Return to School
- Your child can return to child care or school after the stools are formed and the fever is gone. The school-aged child can return if the diarrhea is mild and the child has good control over loose stools.

See More Appropriate Topic (Instead of This One) If
- Vomiting is present along with diarrhea (see Chapter 29, Vomiting With Diarrhea)

When to Call Your Doctor

Call 911 Now (Your Child May Need an Ambulance) If
- Not moving or too weak to stand

Call Your Doctor Now (Night or Day) If
- Your child looks or acts very sick
- Signs of dehydration (eg, no urine longer than 8 hours, no tears with crying, very dry mouth)
- Blood in the stool
- Weak immune system (eg, sickle cell disease, HIV, chemotherapy, organ transplant, chronic steroids)
- Abdominal pain present longer than 2 hours
- Vomiting clear liquids 3 or more times
- Child is younger than 1 month with 3 or more diarrhea stools (mucus, bad odor, increased looseness)
- Passed more than 8 diarrhea stools in the last 8 hours
- Severe diarrhea while taking a medicine that could cause diarrhea (eg, antibiotics)
- Fever above 104°F (40°C) and not improved 2 hours after fever medicine
- Child is younger than 12 weeks with fever above 100.4°F (38.0°C) rectally (CAUTION: Do NOT give your baby any fever medicine before being seen.)

Call Your Doctor Within 24 Hours (Between 9:00 am and 4:00 pm) If
- You think your child needs to be seen
- Pus in the stool present for more than 2 days
- Loss of bowel control in a toilet-trained child occurs 3 or more times
- Fever present for more than 3 days
- Close contact with person or animal who has bacterial diarrhea
- Contact with reptile (snake, lizard, turtle) in previous 14 days
- Travel to country at risk for bacterial diarrhea within past month

Call Your Doctor During Weekday Office Hours If
- You have other questions or concerns
- Diarrhea persists more than 2 weeks
- Loose stools are a chronic problem

Parent Care at Home If
- Mild diarrhea (probably viral gastroenteritis) and you don't think your child needs to be seen

Home Care Advice for Diarrhea

1. **Reassurance**
   - Most diarrhea is caused by a viral infection of the intestines.
   - Diarrhea is the body's way of getting rid of the germs.
   - Here are some tips on how to keep ahead of the fluid losses.
2. **Mild Diarrhea**
   - Continue regular diet.
   - Eat more starchy foods (eg, cereal, crackers, rice).
   - Drink more fluids. Formula or milk are good balanced fluids for diarrhea (EXCEPTION: Avoid all fruit juices and soft drinks because they make diarrhea worse).
3. **Formula-Fed Infants With Frequent, Watery Diarrhea: Start Oral Rehydration Solution (ORS)**
   - ORS (eg, Pedialyte, store brand) is a special electrolyte solution that can prevent dehydration. It's readily available in supermarkets and drugstores.
   - Start ORS for frequent, watery diarrhea (Note: formula is fine for average diarrhea).
   - Use ORS alone for 4 to 6 hours to prevent dehydration. Offer unlimited amounts.
   - If ORS is not available, use formula prepared in the usual way (unlimited amounts) until you can get some.
   - Avoid Jell-O water, sports drinks, and fruit juice.
4. **Returning to Formula**
   - Go back to formula by 6 hours at the latest (Reason: child needs the calories).
   - Use formula prepared in the usual way (Reason: it contains adequate water).
   - Offer formula more frequently than you normally do.
   - **Lactose:** Regular formula is fine for most diarrhea. Lactose-free formulas (soy formula) are only needed for watery diarrhea persisting more than 3 days.
   - **Extra ORS:** Also give 2 to 4 oz (30 to 120 mL) of ORS after every large, watery stool.

5. **Solids**
   - **Infants Older Than 4 Months:** Continue solids (eg, rice cereal, strained bananas, mashed potatoes).
6. **Breastfed Infants With Frequent, Watery Diarrhea**
   - Continue breastfeeding at more frequent intervals. Continue solids as for formula fed.
   - Offer 2 to 4 oz (60 to 120 mL) ORS (eg, Pedialyte) after every large, watery stool (especially if urine is dark) in addition to breastfeeding.
7. **Children Older Than 1 Year With Frequent, Watery Diarrhea**
   - **Fluids:** Offer unlimited fluids. If taking solids, give water or half-strength Gatorade. If child refuses solids, give milk or formula.
   - Avoid all fruit juices and soft drinks (Reason: make diarrhea worse).
   - ORS (eg, Pedialyte) is rarely needed, but for severe diarrhea, also give 4 to 8 oz (120 to 240 mL) of ORS after every large, watery stool.
   - **Solids:** Starchy foods are absorbed best. Give dried cereals, oatmeal, bread, crackers, noodles, mashed potatoes, or rice. Pretzels or salty crackers can help meet sodium needs.
8. **Probiotics**
   - Probiotics contain healthy bacteria (lactobacilli) that can replace unhealthy bacteria in the gastrointestinal tract.
   - **Yogurt** is the easiest source of probiotics. If your child is older than 12 months, give 2 to 6 oz (60 to 180 mL) of yogurt twice daily (Note: today, almost all yogurts are "active culture").
   - Probiotic supplements in granules, tablets, or capsules are also available in health food stores.
9. **Diaper Rash:** Wash buttocks after each stool to prevent a bad diaper rash. Consider applying a protective ointment (eg, petroleum jelly) around the anus to protect the skin.
10. **Contagiousness:** Your child can return to child care or school after the stools are formed and the fever is gone. The school-aged child can return if the diarrhea is mild and the child has good control over loose stools.

11. **Expected Course:** Viral diarrhea lasts 5 to 14 days. Severe diarrhea only occurs on the first 1 or 2 days, but loose stools can persist for 1 to 2 weeks.

12. **Call Your Doctor If**
    - Signs of dehydration occur.
    - Diarrhea persists more than 2 weeks.
    - Your child becomes worse.

> **And remember, contact your doctor if your child develops any of the "Call Your Doctor" symptoms.**

Chapter 29

Vomiting With Diarrhea

Definition

- Vomiting is the forceful emptying (throwing up) of a large portion of the stomach's contents through the mouth.
- Nausea and abdominal discomfort usually precede each bout of vomiting.
- Vomiting and diarrhea together is covered by this topic (EXCEPTION: If vomiting is resolved, use Chapter 28, Diarrhea).

Causes
- **Main Cause:** Stomach and intestinal infection (gastroenteritis) from a stomach virus (eg, rotavirus). The illness starts with vomiting but diarrhea usually follows within 12 to 24 hours.
- Food poisoning from toxins produced by bacteria growing in poorly refrigerated foods (eg, *Staphylococcus* toxin in egg salad, *Bacillus cereus* toxin in rice dishes).

Severity of Vomiting
The following is an arbitrary attempt to classify vomiting by risk for dehydration:
- **Mild:** 1 to 2 times a day.
- **Moderate:** 3 to 7 times a day.
- **Severe:** Vomits everything or nearly everything, or 8 or more times a day.
- Severity relates even more to the length of time that the particular severity level has persisted. At the beginning of a vomiting illness (especially following food poisoning), it's common for a child to vomit everything for 3 or 4 hours and then become stable with mild or moderate vomiting.
- Watery stools in combination with vomiting carry the greatest risk for causing dehydration.
- The younger the child, the greater the risk for dehydration.

How to Recognize Dehydration

- Dehydration means that the body has lost excessive fluids, usually from vomiting or diarrhea. An associated weight loss of more than 3% is required. In general, mild diarrhea, mild vomiting, or a mild decrease in fluid intake does not cause dehydration.
- Dehydration is the most important complication of diarrhea.
- The following are signs of dehydration:
  - Decreased urination (no urine in more than 8 hours) occurs early in the process of dehydration. So does a dark-yellow, concentrated yellow. If the urine is light straw colored, your child is not dehydrated.
  - Dry tongue and inside of the mouth. Dry lips are not helpful.
  - Dry eyes with decreased or absent tears.
  - In infants, a depressed or sunken soft spot.
  - Delayed capillary refill longer than 2 seconds. This refers to the return of a pink color to the thumbnail after you press it and make it pale. Ask your child's doctor to teach you how to do this test.
  - Irritable, tired out, or acting ill. If your child is alert, happy, and playful, he is not dehydrated.
  - A child with severe dehydration becomes too weak to stand or very dizzy if he tries to stand.

Return to School

- Your child can return to child care or school after vomiting and fever are gone.

See More Appropriate Topic (Instead of This One) If

- Vomiting without diarrhea (see Chapter 30, Vomiting Without Diarrhea)
- Diarrhea is main symptom (vomiting is resolved) (see Chapter 28, Diarrhea)

When to Call Your Doctor

Call 911 Now (Your Child May Need an Ambulance) If
- Unresponsive or difficult to awaken
- Not moving or too weak to stand

Call Your Doctor Now (Night or Day) If
- Your child looks or acts very sick
- Signs of dehydration (very dry mouth, no tears, and no urine in more than 8 hours)
- Blood in the stool
- Blood in the vomit that's not from a nosebleed
- Bile (bright yellow or green) in the vomit
- Abdominal pain is also present (EXCEPTION: Abdominal pain or crying just before and improved by vomiting is quite common.)
- Appendicitis suspected (eg, pain low on right side, won't jump, prefers to lie still)
- Poisoning with a plant, medicine, or other chemical suspected
- Child is younger than 12 weeks with vomiting 2 or more times (EXCEPTION: spitting up)
- Child younger than 12 months who has vomited Pedialyte (or other brand of oral rehydration solution) 3 or more times and also has watery diarrhea
- Receiving Pedialyte (or clear fluids if older than 1 year) and vomits everything longer than 8 hours
- Weak immune system (eg, sickle cell disease, HIV, chemotherapy, organ transplant, chronic steroids)
- Vomiting an essential medicine
- Fever above 104°F (40°C) and not improved 2 hours after fever medicine
- Child is younger than 12 weeks with fever above 100.4°F (38.0°C) rectally (CAUTION: Do NOT give your baby any fever medicine before being seen.)

Call Your Doctor Within 24 Hours (Between 9:00 am and 4:00 pm) If

- You think your child needs to be seen
- Has vomited longer than 24 hours
- Fever present for more than 3 days

Call Your Doctor During Weekday Office Hours If

- You have other questions or concerns
- Vomiting is a recurrent chronic problem

Parent Care at Home If

- Mild to moderate vomiting with diarrhea (probably viral gastroenteritis) and you don't think your child needs to be seen

Home Care Advice for Vomiting With Diarrhea

1. **Reassurance**
   - Most vomiting is caused by a viral infection of the stomach and intestines or by food poisoning.
   - Vomiting is the body's way of protecting the lower intestinal tract.
   - When vomiting and diarrhea occur together, treat the vomiting. Don't do anything special for the diarrhea.

2. **For Bottle-fed Infants, Offer Oral Rehydration Solution (ORS) for 8 Hours**
   - ORS (eg, Pedialyte, store brand) is a special electrolyte solution that can prevent dehydration. It's readily available in supermarkets and drugstores.
   - For vomiting once, continue regular formula.
   - For vomiting more than once, offer ORS for 8 hours. If ORS is not available, use formula.
   - Spoon or syringe feed small amounts of ORS—1 to 2 teaspoons (5 to 10 mL) every 5 minutes.
   - After 4 hours without vomiting, double the amount.
   - After 8 hours without vomiting, return to regular formula.
   - For infants older than 4 months, also return to cereal and strained bananas.
   - Return to normal diet in 24 to 48 hours.

3. **For Breastfed Infants, Reduce the Amount Per Feeding**
   - If infant vomits once, nurse 1 side every 1 to 2 hours.
   - If infant vomits more than once, nurse for 5 minutes every 30 to 60 minutes. After 4 hours without vomiting, return to regular breastfeeding.
   - If infant continues to vomit, switch to ORS (eg, Pedialyte) for 4 hours.
   - Spoon or syringe feed small amounts of ORS—1 to 2 teaspoons (5 to 10 mL) every 5 minutes.
   - After 4 hours without vomiting, return to regular breastfeeding. Start with small feedings of 5 minutes every 30 minutes and increase as tolerated.

4. **For Older Children (Older Than 1 Year), Offer Small Amounts of Clear Fluids for 8 Hours**
   - **ORS:** Vomiting with watery diarrhea needs ORS (eg, Pedialyte). If child refuses ORS, use half-strength Gatorade.
   - Give small amounts—2 to 3 teaspoons (10 to 15 mL) every 5 minutes.
   - After 4 hours without vomiting, increase the amount.
   - After 8 hours without vomiting, return to regular fluids.
   - **Solids:** After 8 hours without vomiting, add solids.
     - Limit solids to bland foods. Starchy foods are easiest to digest.
     - Start with saltine crackers, white bread, cereals, rice, and mashed potatoes.
     - Return to normal diet in 24 to 48 hours.

5. **Avoid Medicines**
   - Discontinue all nonessential medicines for 8 hours (Reason: usually make vomiting worse).
   - **Fever:** Fevers usually don't need any medicine. For higher fevers, consider acetaminophen (eg, Tylenol) suppositories. Never give oral ibuprofen (eg, Advil); it is a stomach irritant.
   - **Call your doctor if** your child is vomiting an essential medicine.

6. **Contagiousness:** Your child can return to child care or school after vomiting and fever are gone.

7. **Expected Course:** Moderate vomiting usually stops in 12 to 24 hours. Mild vomiting (1 to 2 times a day) with diarrhea can continue intermittently for up to a week.

8. **Call Your Doctor If**
   - Vomiting becomes severe (vomits everything) longer than 8 hours.
   - Vomiting persists longer than 24 hours.
   - Signs of dehydration.
   - Diarrhea becomes severe.
   - Your child becomes worse.

And remember, contact your doctor if your child develops any of the "Call Your Doctor" symptoms.

Chapter 30

Vomiting Without Diarrhea

Definition

- Vomiting is the forceful emptying (throwing up) of a large portion of the stomach's contents through the mouth.
- Nausea and abdominal discomfort usually precede each bout of vomiting.

Causes
- **Main Cause:** Stomach infection (gastritis) from a stomach virus (eg, rotavirus). The illness starts with vomiting but diarrhea usually follows within 12 to 24 hours.
- Food poisoning from toxins produced by bacteria growing in poorly refrigerated foods (eg, *Staphylococcus* toxin in egg salad, *Bacillus cereus* toxin in rice dishes).
- **Serious Causes:** If vomiting persists as an isolated symptom (without diarrhea) for more than 24 hours, more serious causes must be considered. Examples are appendicitis, kidney infection, meningitis, and head injury.
- Vomiting can also be triggered by hard coughing. This is common, especially in children with reflux.

Severity of Vomiting
The following is an arbitrary attempt to classify vomiting by risk for dehydration:
- **Mild:** 1 to 2 times a day.
- **Moderate:** 3 to 7 times a day.
- **Severe:** Vomits everything or nearly everything, or 8 or more times a day.

- Severity relates even more to the length of time that the particular severity level has persisted. At the beginning of a vomiting illness (especially following food poisoning), it's common for a child to vomit everything for 3 or 4 hours and then become stable with mild or moderate vomiting.
- The younger the child, the greater the risk for dehydration.

Return to School
- Your child can return to child care or school after vomiting and fever are gone.

See More Appropriate Topic (Instead of This One) If
- Vomiting occurs with diarrhea (see Chapter 29, Vomiting With Diarrhea)
- Vomiting only occurs while coughing (see Chapter 23, Cough)
- Diarrhea is the main symptom (see Chapter 28, Diarrhea)

When to Call Your Doctor

Call 911 Now (Your Child May Need an Ambulance) If
- Unresponsive or difficult to awaken
- Not moving or too weak to stand

Call Your Doctor Now (Night or Day) If
- Your child looks or acts very sick
- Confused (delirious)
- Stiff neck or bulging soft spot
- Headache
- Signs of dehydration (very dry mouth, no tears, and no urine in more than 8 hours)
- Blood in the vomit that's not from a nosebleed
- Bile (bright yellow or green) in the vomit
- Abdominal pain is also present (EXCEPTION: Abdominal pain or crying just before and improved by vomiting is quite common.)
- Appendicitis suspected (eg, pain low on right side, won't jump, prefers to lie still)

- Diabetes suspected (excessive drinking, frequent urination, weight loss)
- Poisoning with a plant, medicine, or other chemical suspected
- Child is younger than 12 weeks with vomiting 2 or more times (EXCEPTION: spitting up)
- Receiving Pedialyte (or clear fluids if older than 1 year) and vomits everything longer than 8 hours
- High-risk child (eg, diabetes mellitus, abdominal injury, head injury)
- Weak immune system (eg, sickle cell disease, HIV, chemotherapy, organ transplant, chronic steroids)
- Vomiting an essential medicine
- Fever above 104°F (40°C) and not improved 2 hours after fever medicine
- Child is younger than 12 weeks with fever above 100.4°F (38.0°C) rectally (CAUTION: Do NOT give your baby any fever medicine before being seen.)

Call Your Doctor Within 24 Hours (Between 9:00 am and 4:00 pm) If
- You think your child needs to be seen
- Has vomited longer than 24 hours
- Fever present for more than 3 days
- Fever returns after gone for longer than 24 hours

Call Your Doctor During Weekday Office Hours If
- You have other questions or concerns
- Vomiting is a recurrent chronic problem

Parent Care at Home If
- Mild to moderate vomiting (probably viral gastritis) and you don't think your child needs to be seen

Home Care Advice for Vomiting

1. **Reassurance**
   - Most vomiting is caused by a viral infection of the stomach or mild food poisoning.
   - Vomiting is the body's way of protecting the lower intestinal tract.
   - Fortunately, vomiting illnesses are usually brief.

2. **For Bottle-fed Infants, Offer Oral Rehydration Solution (ORS) for 8 Hours**
   - ORS (eg, Pedialyte, store brand) is a special electrolyte solution that can prevent dehydration. It's readily available in supermarkets and drugstores.
   - For vomiting once, continue regular formula.
   - For vomiting more than once, offer ORS for 8 hours. If ORS is not available, use formula.
   - Spoon or syringe feed small amounts of ORS—1 to 2 teaspoons (5 to 10 mL) every 5 minutes.
   - After 4 hours without vomiting, double the amount.
   - After 8 hours without vomiting, return to regular formula.
   - For infants older than 4 months, also return to cereal and strained bananas.
   - Return to normal diet in 24 to 48 hours.

3. **For Breastfed Infants, Reduce the Amount Per Feeding**
   - If infant vomits once, nurse 1 side every 1 to 2 hours.
   - If infant vomits more than once, nurse for 5 minutes every 30 to 60 minutes. After 4 hours without vomiting, return to regular breastfeeding.
   - If infant continues to vomit, switch to ORS (eg, Pedialyte) for 4 hours.
   - Spoon or syringe feed small amounts of ORS—1 to 2 teaspoons (5 to 10 mL) every 5 minutes.
   - After 4 hours without vomiting, return to regular breastfeeding. Start with small feedings of 5 minutes every 30 minutes and increase as tolerated.

4. **For Children Older Than 1 Year, Offer Small Amounts of Clear Fluids for 8 Hours**
   - Water or ice chips are best for vomiting in older children (Reason: water is directly absorbed across the stomach wall).
   - **ORS:** If child vomits water, offer ORS (eg, Pedialyte). If child refuses ORS, use half-strength Gatorade.
   - Give small amounts—2 to 3 teaspoons (10 to 15 mL) every 5 minutes.
   - **Other Options:** Half-strength flat lemon-lime soda, popsicles, or ORS frozen pops.
   - After 4 hours without vomiting, increase the amount.
   - After 8 hours without vomiting, return to regular fluids.
   - CAUTION: If vomiting continues for more than 12 hours, switch to ORS or half-strength Gatorade.
   - **Solids:** After 8 hours without vomiting, add solids.
     - Limit solids to bland foods. Starchy foods are easiest to digest.
     - Start with saltine crackers, white bread, cereals, rice, and mashed potatoes.
     - Return to normal diet in 24 to 48 hours.
5. **Avoid Medicines**
   - Discontinue all nonessential medicines for 8 hours (Reason: usually make vomiting worse).
   - **Fever:** Fevers usually don't need any medicine. For higher fevers, consider acetaminophen (eg, Tylenol) suppositories. Never give oral ibuprofen (eg, Advil); it is a stomach irritant.
   - **Call your doctor** if your child is vomiting an essential medicine.
6. **Sleep:** Help your child go to sleep for a few hours (Reason: sleep often empties the stomach and relieves the need to vomit). Your child doesn't have to drink anything if she feels very nauseated.
7. **Contagiousness:** Your child can return to child care or school after vomiting and fever are gone.
8. **Expected Course:** Vomiting from viral gastritis usually stops in 12 to 24 hours. Mild vomiting with nausea may last up to 3 days.

9. **Call Your Doctor If**
   - Vomiting becomes severe (vomits everything) longer than 8 hours.
   - Vomiting persists longer than 24 hours.
   - Signs of dehydration.
   - Your child becomes worse.

And remember, contact your doctor if your child develops any of the "Call Your Doctor" symptoms.

Part 8

Genital or Urinary
Symptoms

Chapter 31

Urination Pain

Definition

- Discomfort (pain, burning, or stinging) when passing urine.
- In children too young to talk, suspect pain if your child begins to cry regularly while passing urine.
- Urgency (can't wait) and frequency (passing small amounts) of urination may be associated symptoms.

Causes
- **Main Cause in Young Girls:** An irritation and redness of the vulva and opening of the urethra from bubble bath, shampoo, or soapy bath water (soap vulvitis).
- Any boy with painful urination needs his urine checked. Occasionally in young boys the urine is normal and the pain is caused by an irritation of the opening of the penis. In teenaged boys, pain can be due to inflammation of the urethra caused by a sexually transmitted infection.
- Bladder or kidney infections (urinary tract infections) are possible at any age.

Return to School
- Even if your child has a bladder infection, it is not contagious. Your child does not need to miss any school or child care.

When to Call Your Doctor

Call 911 Now (Your Child May Need an Ambulance) If

- Not moving or too weak to stand

Call Your Doctor Now (Night or Day) If

- Your child looks or acts very sick
- Can't pass urine or only can pass a few drops
- Blood in urine
- Severe pain with urination
- Fever is present
- Abdominal, side, or back pain

Call Your Doctor Within 24 Hours (Between 9:00 am and 4:00 pm) If

- Painful urination, but none of the symptoms described herein (Reason: possible bladder infection)

Home Care Advice for Soap Vulvitis
(Pending Talking With Your Doctor)

1. **Definition:** Soap vulvitis is the number 1 cause of pain with urination in young girls.
   - Burning or stinging with passing urine.
   - Vaginal itching or irritation may also be present.
   - Prepubertal girl younger than 10 years.
   - Uses bubble bath, bathes in soapy water, or washes genitals with soap.
   - To be sure she doesn't have a bladder or kidney infection, she usually needs to have her urine checked. The following treatment will reduce symptoms while awaiting your appointment:

2. **Baking Soda/Warm Water Soaks**
   - Soak for 20 minutes to remove irritants and to promote healing.
   - Add 2 oz (60 mL) baking soda per tub of warm water (Reason: baking soda is better than vinegar for girls not into puberty).
   - During soaks, be sure she spreads her legs and allows the water to cleanse the genital area.
   - Repeat baking soda soak treatment 2 times per day for 2 days.

3. **Avoid Soaps:** Avoid bubble bath, soap, and shampoo to the vulva because they are irritants. Only use warm water to cleanse the vulva or baby oil to remove secretions.

4. **Increased Fluids:** Give extra fluids to drink (Reason: to produce a dilute, nonirritating urine).

5. **Pain Medicine:** To reduce painful urination, give acetaminophen (eg, Tylenol) every 4 hours OR ibuprofen (eg, Advil) every 6 hours as needed (see dosage table in Appendix A or E).

6. **Contagiousness:** Even if your child has a bladder infection, it is not contagious. Your child does not need to miss any school or child care.

7. **Call Your Doctor If**
   - Pain with urination becomes severe.
   - Fever occurs.
   - Your child becomes worse.

> **And remember, contact your doctor if your child develops any of the "Call Your Doctor" symptoms.**

Chapter 32

Vaginal Itching or Irritation

Definition

- Genital-area burning or itching in young girls
- No pain or burning with urination

Cause
- **Main Cause in Young Girls:** A soap irritation of the vulva or outer vagina (soap vulvitis) from bubble bath, shampoo, or other soap.
- Soap vulvitis occurs exclusively prior to puberty.
- Occasionally, it is caused by poor hygiene or back-to-front wiping.
- If the vagina becomes secondarily infected, a vaginal discharge will occur.

See More Appropriate Topic (Instead of This One) If
- Pain or burning with urination (see Chapter 31, Urination Pain)

When to Call Your Doctor

Call Your Doctor Now (Night or Day) If

- Your child looks or acts very sick
- Could be from sexual abuse
- Vaginal bleeding

Call Your Doctor Within 24 Hours (Between 9:00 am and 4:00 pm) If

- You think your child needs to be seen
- Vaginal discharge
- Fever is present

Call Your Doctor During Weekday Office Hours If

- You have other questions or concerns
- Child is older than 10 years (Reason: soap vulvitis is unusual)
- Vaginal irritation persists on treatment more than 2 days

Parent Care at Home If

- Probable soap vulvitis and you don't think your child needs to be seen

Home Care Advice for Soap Vulvitis

1. **Reassurance**
   - Soap (especially bubble bath) is the most common cause of genital itching in young girls.
   - The vulva is very sensitive to the drying effect of soap.
   - After puberty, soap can be tolerated.

2. **Baking Soda/Warm Water Soaks**
   - Soak for 20 minutes to remove irritants and to promote healing.
   - Add 2 oz (60 mL) baking soda per tub of warm water (Reason: baking soda is better than vinegar for girls not into puberty).
   - During soaks, be sure she spreads her legs and allows the water to cleanse the genital area.
   - Repeat baking soda soak treatment 2 times per day for 2 days.

3. **Steroid Cream:** Apply small amount of 1% hydrocortisone cream (no prescription needed) to the genital area after soaks for 1 or 2 days.

4. **Avoid Soaps:** Avoid bubble bath, soap, and shampoo to the vulva because they are irritants. Only use warm water to cleanse the vulva or baby oil to remove secretions.

5. **Expected Course:** If the symptoms are caused by soap vulvitis, they should all clear within 1 to 2 days with proper treatment.

6. **Call Your Doctor If**
   - Irritation persists on treatment longer than 48 hours.
   - Vaginal discharge or bleeding occurs.
   - Passing urine becomes painful.
   - Your child becomes worse.

> **And remember, contact your doctor if your child develops any of the "Call Your Doctor" symptoms.**

Part 9

Arm or Leg
Symptoms

Chapter 33

Arm Injury

Definition

- Injuries to arm (shoulder to fingers)
- Injuries to a bone, muscle, joint, or ligament

Types of Arm Injuries

- **Fractures (Broken Bones):** A broken collarbone (clavicle) is the most common fracture of childhood. These are easy to recognize because the collarbone is tender to touch and the child is unwilling to raise the arm upward.
- **Dislocations (Bone Out of Joint):** A pulled elbow is the most common dislocation of childhood. It's caused by an adult suddenly pulling or lifting a child by the arm. It happens mainly from 1 to 4 years of age. It is easy to recognize because the child holds his arm as if it were in a sling with the elbow bent and the palm down.
- **Sprains:** Stretches and tears of ligaments.
- **Strains:** Stretches and tears of muscles (eg, pulled muscle).
- Muscle overuse injuries from sports or exercise.
- Muscle bruise from a direct blow.
- Bone bruise from a direct blow.

Pain Severity Scale

- **Mild:** Doesn't interfere with normal activities
- **Moderate:** Interferes with normal activities or awakens from sleep
- **Severe:** Excruciating pain, unable to do any normal activities, incapacitated by pain

See More Appropriate Topic (Instead of This One) If

- Only has cuts, scrapes, or bruises (see Chapter 37, Cuts, Scrapes, or Bruises [Skin Injury])

When to Call Your Doctor

Call 911 Now (Your Child May Need an Ambulance) If
- Serious injury with multiple fractures
- Major bleeding that can't be stopped

Call Your Doctor Now (Night or Day) If
- You think your child has a serious injury
- Looks like a broken bone or dislocated joint
- Swollen elbow or any large swelling
- Skin beyond the injury is pale or blue
- Skin is split open or gaping and may need stitches
- Child is younger than 1 year
- Bicycle spoke or washing machine wringer injury
- Pain is SEVERE (and not improved after 2 hours of pain medicine)
- Unable to move arm or shoulder normally (especially if someone pulled on the arm)
- Young child and cries when you try to move the shoulder (collarbone fracture suspected)
- Joint nearest the injury can't be moved fully (opened and closed)

Call Your Doctor Within 24 Hours (Between 9:00 am and 4:00 pm) If
- You think your child needs to be seen
- Pain not improved after 3 days

Call Your Doctor During Weekday Office Hours If
- You have other questions or concerns
- Pain lasts more than 2 weeks

Parent Care at Home If
- Bruised muscle or bone from direct blow
- Pain in muscle (probably from mild pulled muscle)
- Pain around joint (probably from mild stretched ligament)

Home Care Advice for Minor Arm Injuries

1. **Reassurance:** Bruised muscles or bones can be treated at home.
2. **Pain Medicine:** Give acetaminophen (eg, Tylenol) or ibuprofen (eg, Advil) as needed for pain relief (see dosage table in Appendix A or E). Ibuprofen is more effective for this type of pain.
3. **Local Cold:** For bruises or swelling, apply a cold pack or ice bag wrapped in a wet cloth to the area for 20 minutes per hour. Repeat for 4 consecutive hours (Reason: reduce the bleeding and pain).
4. **Local Heat:** After 48 hours, apply a warm, wet washcloth or heating pad for 10 minutes 3 times per day to help absorb the blood.
5. **Rest**
   - Rest the injured part as much as possible for 48 hours.
   - For pulled muscles, teach your youngster about stretching exercises and strength training.
6. **Expected Course:** Pain and swelling usually peak on day 2 or 3. Swelling is usually gone by 7 days. Pain may take 2 weeks to completely resolve.
7. **Call Your Doctor If**
   - Pain becomes severe.
   - Pain is not improving after 3 days.
   - Pain lasts more than 2 weeks.
   - Your child becomes worse.

> **And remember, contact your doctor if your child develops any of the "Call Your Doctor" symptoms.**

Chapter 34

Arm Pain

Definition

- Pain in the arms (shoulder to fingers).
- Includes shoulder, elbow, wrist, and finger joints.
- The pain is not caused by a known injury.
- Minor muscle strain and overuse injury are covered in this topic.

Causes
- Arm pains are unusual.
- **Main Causes:** Strained muscles from overuse injury (eg, excessive throwing or swimming).
- Brief pains (1 to 15 minutes) are usually caused by muscle spasms. These usually occur in the hand and follow prolonged writing or typing.
- Continuous acute pains (hours to 7 days) are usually caused by over-strenuous activities or forgotten muscle injuries during the preceding day. These are most common in the shoulder area.
- Mild muscle aches also occur with many viral illnesses.
- **Serious Causes:** Fractures, arthritis (joint infection), and neuritis (nerve infection).

See More Appropriate Topic (Instead of This One) If
- Follows injury (see Chapter 33, Arm Injury)

When to Call Your Doctor

Call 911 Now (Your Child May Need an Ambulance) If

- Not moving or too weak to stand

Call Your Doctor Now (Night or Day) If

- Your child looks or acts very sick
- Can't use arm normally
- Fever is present
- Can't move a joint normally
- Swollen joint
- Bright red area on skin
- Muscle weakness (loss of strength)
- Numbness (loss of sensation) present longer than 1 hour
- Severe pain or cries when arm touched or moved

Call Your Doctor Within 24 Hours (Between 9:00 am and 4:00 pm) If

- You think your child needs to be seen

Call Your Doctor During Weekday Office Hours If

- You have other questions or concerns
- Cause of arm pain is uncertain
- Arm pain present more than 7 days
- Arm pains or muscle cramps are a recurrent chronic problem

Parent Care at Home If

- Caused by strained muscles from excessive use
- Cause is obvious and harmless (eg, sliver that's removed, a recent shot)

Home Care Advice for Overuse Injury (Strained Muscles)

1. **Reassurance:** Strained muscles are very common following vigorous activity (overuse injury) (eg, repeatedly throwing a ball). You can treat them at home.

2. **Local Cold:** Apply a cold pack or ice bag wrapped in a wet cloth to the sore muscles for 20 minutes several times on the first 2 days.

3. **Pain Medicine:** Give acetaminophen (eg, Tylenol) or ibuprofen (eg, Advil) as needed for pain relief (see dosage table in Appendix A or E).

4. **Hot Bath:** If stiffness persists longer than 48 hours, have your child relax in a hot bath for 20 minutes 2 times per day, and gently exercise the involved part under water.

5. **Expected Course:** A strained muscle hurts for 2 or 3 days. The pain often peaks on day 2. Following severe overuse, the pain may last a week.

6. **Call Your Doctor If**
   - Fever or swollen joint occurs.
   - Pain caused by work or exercise persists more than 7 days.
   - Pain becomes worse.

> **And remember, contact your doctor if your child develops any of the "Call Your Doctor" symptoms.**

Chapter 35

Leg Injury

Definition

- Injuries to leg (hip to toes)
- Injuries to a bone, muscle, joint, or ligament

Types of Leg Injuries
- Fractures (broken bones).
- Dislocations (bone out of joint).
- **Sprains:** Stretches and tears of ligaments. A sprained ankle is the most common ligament injury of the leg. It's usually caused by turning the ankle inward. The main symptoms are pain and swelling of the outside of the ankle.
- **Strains:** Stretches and tears of muscles (eg, pulled muscle).
- Muscle overuse injuries from sports or exercise (eg, shin splints of lower leg).
- Muscle bruise from a direct blow (eg, thigh muscles).
- Bone bruise from a direct blow (eg, hip).

Pain Severity Scale
- **Mild:** Doesn't interfere with normal activities
- **Moderate:** Interferes with normal activities or awakens from sleep
- **Severe:** Excruciating pain, unable to do any normal activities, incapacitated by pain

See More Appropriate Topic (Instead of This One) If
- Only has cuts, scrapes, or bruises (see Chapter 37, Cuts, Scrapes, or Bruises [Skin Injury])

When to Call Your Doctor

Call 911 Now (Your Child May Need an Ambulance) If
- Serious injury with multiple fractures
- Major bleeding that can't be stopped

Call Your Doctor Now (Night or Day) If
- You think your child has a serious injury
- Looks like a broken bone or dislocated joint
- Large swelling
- Skin beyond the injury is pale or blue
- Skin is split open or gaping and may need stitches
- Child is younger than 1 year
- Bicycle spoke or washing machine wringer injury
- Pain is SEVERE (and not improved after 2 hours of pain medicine)
- Won't stand or walk
- Has a limp when walking
- Unable to move leg or hip normally
- Joint nearest the injury can't be moved fully (opened and closed)
- Knee injury with a "snap" or "pop" felt at the time of impact

Call Your Doctor Within 24 Hours (Between 9:00 am and 4:00 pm) If
- You think your child needs to be seen
- Pain not improved after 3 days

Call Your Doctor During Weekday Office Hours If
- You have other questions or concerns
- No tetanus shot in more than 5 years for DIRTY cuts (more than 10 years for CLEAN cuts)
- Pain lasts more than 2 weeks

Parent Care at Home If
- Bruised muscle or bone from direct blow
- Pain in muscle (probably from mild pulled muscle)
- Pain around joint (probably from mild stretched ligament)

Home Care Advice for Minor Leg Injuries

1. **Treatment of Pulled Muscle, Bruised Muscle, or Bruised Bone**
   - **Reassurance:** Bruised muscles or bones can be treated at home.
   - **Pain Medicine:** Give acetaminophen (eg, Tylenol) or ibuprofen (eg, Advil) as needed for pain relief (see dosage table in Appendix A or E). Ibuprofen is more effective for this type of pain.
   - **Local Cold:** For bruises or swelling, apply a cold pack or ice bag wrapped in a wet cloth to the area for 20 minutes per hour. Repeat for 4 consecutive hours (Reason: reduce the bleeding and pain).
   - **Local Heat:** After 48 hours apply a warm, wet washcloth or heating pad for 10 minutes 3 times per day to help absorb the blood.
   - **Rest:** Rest the injured part as much as possible for 48 hours.
   - For pulled muscles, teach your youngster about stretching exercises and strength training.

2. **Treatment of Mild Sprains (Stretched Ligaments) of Ankle or Knee**
   - **First Aid:** Immediate compression and ice to reduce bleeding, swelling, and pain.
   - Treat with RICE (rest, ice, compression, and elevation) for the first 24 to 48 hours.
   - Apply compression with a snug, elastic bandage for 48 hours. Numbness, tingling, or increased pain means the bandage is too tight.
   - Apply a cold pack or ice bag wrapped in a wet cloth to the area for 20 minutes per hour. Repeat for 4 consecutive hours.
   - Give acetaminophen (eg, Tylenol) or ibuprofen (eg, Advil) as needed for pain relief (see dosage table in Appendix A or E). Continue for at least 48 hours.
   - Keep injured ankle or knee elevated and at rest for 24 hours.
   - After 24 hours, allow any activity that doesn't cause pain.

3. **Expected Course:** Pain and swelling usually peak on day 2 or 3. Swelling is usually gone by 7 days. Pain may take 2 weeks to completely resolve.

4. **Call Your Doctor If**
   - Pain becomes severe.
   - Pain is not improving after 3 days.
   - Pain lasts more than 2 weeks.
   - Your child becomes worse.

> **And remember, contact your doctor if your child develops any of the "Call Your Doctor" symptoms.**

Chapter 36

Leg Pain

Definition

- Pain in the legs (hip to toes).
- Includes hip, knee, ankle, and toe joints.
- The pain is not caused by a known injury.
- Minor muscle strain and overuse injury are covered in this chapter.

Causes

- **Main Causes:** Muscle spasms (cramps) and strained muscles from overuse injury (eg, excessive running or jumping). Up to 50% of all injuries seen in pediatric sports medicine are related to overuse.
- **Muscle Cramps:** Brief pains (1 to 15 minutes) are usually caused by muscle spasms (cramps). Foot or calf muscles are especially prone to cramps that occur during exercise or that awaken your child from sleep. Muscle cramps that occur during exercise are also called heat cramps. They often respond to extra water and salt.
- **Strained Muscles:** Continuous acute pains (hours to 7 days) are usually caused by over-strenuous activities or forgotten muscle injuries during the preceding day. They can occur in arms or legs.
- **Growing Pains:** 10% of healthy children have intermittent, harmless pains that are often referred to as growing pains (although they have nothing to do with growth). Growing pains usually occur in the calf or thigh muscles. They always occur on both sides, not one. They occur late in the day and are probably caused by running and playing hard. They usually last 10 to 30 minutes.
- **Viral Infections:** Muscle aches in both legs are common with viral illness, especially influenza.

- **Serious Causes:** Fractures, deep vein thrombosis, neuritis (nerve infection), and arthritis (joint infection). Septic arthritis (a bacterial infection of any joint space) is a medical emergency. The symptoms are severe joint pain, resistance to any joint movement, and a high fever. Toxic synovitis of the hip is a benign condition that can imitate a septic arthritis of the hip. The symptoms are a limp, moderate pain, and usually no fever. Toxic synovitis tends to occur in toddlers following excessive jumping.

See More Appropriate Topic (Instead of This One) If
- Follows injury (see Chapter 35, Leg Injury)

When to Call Your Doctor

Call 911 Now (Your Child May Need an Ambulance) If
- Not moving or too weak to stand

Call Your Doctor Now (Night or Day) If
- Your child looks or acts very sick
- Can't stand or walk
- Fever and pain in one leg only
- Can't move a joint normally
- Swollen joint
- Calf pain on 1 side lasts longer than 12 hours
- Bright red area on skin
- Muscle weakness or can't stand or walk
- Numbness (loss of sensation) present longer than 1 hour
- Severe pain or cries when leg touched or moved

Call Your Doctor Within 24 Hours (Between 9:00 am and 4:00 pm) If
- You think your child needs to be seen
- Walks abnormally (has a limp)
- Fever and pain in both legs

Call Your Doctor During Weekday Office Hours If
- You have other questions or concerns
- Cause of leg pain is uncertain
- Leg pain present more than 7 days
- Leg pains or muscle cramps are a recurrent chronic problem

Parent Care at Home If

- Caused by muscle cramps in the calf or foot
- Caused by overuse injury (strained muscles)
- Growing pains suspected
- Cause is obvious and harmless (eg, tight new shoes, a recent shot)

Home Care Advice for Muscle Cramps, Strains, and Growing Pains

1. **Treatment for Muscle Cramps**
   - Muscle cramps in the feet or calf muscles occur in one third of children.
   - During attacks, stretch the painful muscle by pulling the foot and toes upward as far as they will go to break the spasm.
   - Stretch the muscle in the direction opposite to how it is being pulled by the cramp or spasm.
   - Apply a cold pack or ice bag wrapped in a wet cloth to the painful muscle for 20 minutes.
   - If these are heat cramps (occurring during exercise on a hot day), give lots of water and sports drink in addition to stretching the muscle and a cold pack.
   - Future attacks may be prevented by daily stretching exercises of the heel cords (stand with the knees straight and stretch the ankles by leaning forward against a wall). Also give the feet more room to move at night by placing a pillow under the covers at the foot of the bed. Also be sure your child gets enough calcium in her diet.

2. **Treatment for Strained Muscles From Excessive Use (Overuse Injury)**
   - Apply a cold pack or ice bag wrapped in a wet cloth to the sore muscles for 20 minutes several times on the first 2 days.
   - Give acetaminophen (eg, Tylenol) or ibuprofen (eg, Advil) as needed for pain relief (see dosage table in Appendix A or E).
   - If stiffness persists longer than 48 hours, have your child relax in a hot bath for 20 minutes twice a day, and gently exercise the involved part under water.

3. **Treatment for Growing Pains**
   - Usually the pains are mild and don't last long, and no treatment is necessary.
   - Massage of the sore muscles can help the pain go away.
   - Give acetaminophen (eg, Tylenol) or ibuprofen (eg, Advil) if the pain lasts more than 30 minutes (see dosage table in Appendix A or E).
   - **Prevention:** Research has show that daily stretching exercises can prevent most growing pains.

4. **Expected Course**
   - Muscle cramps usually last 5 to 30 minutes.
   - Once they resolve, the muscle returns to normal quickly.
   - A strained muscle hurts for 3 to 7 days. The pain often peaks on day 2.
   - Following severe overuse, the pain may last a week.

5. **Call Your Doctor If**
   - Muscle cramps occur more frequently.
   - Child develops a fever, limp, or swollen joint.
   - Pain caused by work or exercise persists more than 7 days.
   - Your child becomes worse.

> **And remember, contact your doctor if your child develops any of the "Call Your Doctor" symptoms.**

Part 10

Skin, Localized
Symptoms

Chapter 37

Cuts, Scrapes, or Bruises (Skin Injury)

Definition

- Cuts, lacerations, gashes, and tears (wounds that go through the skin [dermis] to the fat or muscle tissue)
- Scrapes, abrasions, scratches, and floor burns (superficial wounds that don't go all the way through the skin)
- Bruises (bleeding into the skin) without an overlying cut or scrape

When Sutures (Stitches) Are Needed
- Any cut that is split open or gaping needs sutures.
- Cuts longer than ½ inch (12 mm) usually need sutures.
- On the face, cuts longer than ¼ inch (6 mm) usually need closure with sutures or skin glue.
- Any open wound that may need sutures should be checked and closed as soon as possible (ideally, within 6 hours). There is no cutoff, however, for treating open wounds to prevent wound infections.

Cuts Versus Scratches: Helping You Decide
- The skin (dermis) is 2 mm (about 1/8 inch) thick.
- A cut (laceration) goes through it.
- A scratch or scrape (wide scratch) doesn't go through it.
- Cuts that gape open at rest or with movement need closure to prevent scarring.
- Scrapes and scratches never need closure, no matter how long they are.
- So this distinction is important.

See More Appropriate Topic (Instead of This One) If

- It's a puncture (see Chapter 39, Puncture Wound)
- There's a sliver in the skin (see Chapter 41, Skin, Foreign Body [Splinters])

First Aid Advice for Severe Bleeding

- Place 2 or 3 sterile dressings (or a clean towel or washcloth) over the wound immediately.
- Apply direct pressure to the wound, using your entire hand.
- If bleeding continues, apply pressure more forcefully or to a slightly different spot.
- Act quickly because ongoing blood loss can cause shock.

First Aid Advice for Shock: Lie down with the feet elevated.

First Aid Advice for Penetrating Object: If penetrating object is still in place, don't remove it (Reason: removal could increase internal bleeding).

When to Call Your Doctor

Call 911 Now (Your Child May Need an Ambulance) If

- Major bleeding that can't be stopped (see First Aid Advice)

Call Your Doctor Now (Night or Day) If

- For bleeding, see First Aid Advice
- You think your child has a serious injury
- Bleeding won't stop after 10 minutes of direct pressure
- Deep cut and can see bone or tendons
- Skin is split open or gaping, especially on the face
- Pain is SEVERE (and not improved after 2 hours of pain medicine)
- Child is younger than 1 year
- Dirt or grime in the wound is not removed after 15 minutes of scrubbing
- Wringer-type injury
- Skin loss from bad scrape goes very deep
- Skin loss involves greater than 10% of body surface (Note: the palm of the hand equals 1%)
- Cut or scrape looks infected (redness, red streak, or pus)

Call Your Doctor Within 24 Hours (Between 9:00 am and 4:00 pm) If

- You think your child needs to be seen
- Several bruises occur without any known injury
- Very large bruise follows a minor injury

Call Your Doctor During Weekday Office Hours If

- You have other questions or concerns
- No tetanus shot in more than 5 years for DIRTY cuts (more than 10 years for CLEAN cuts)
- Doesn't heal within 10 days

Parent Care at Home If

- Minor cut, scrape, or bruise and you don't think your child needs to be seen

Home Care Advice for Minor Cuts, Scrapes, or Bruises

1. **Cuts, Scratches, and Scrapes**
   - Apply direct pressure for 10 minutes to stop any bleeding.
   - Wash the wound with soap and water for 5 minutes. (CAUTION: Never soak a wound that might need sutures because it may become more swollen and difficult to close.)
   - Gently scrub out any dirt with a washcloth.
   - Cut off any pieces of loose skin using a fine scissors (cleaned with rubbing alcohol).
   - Apply an antibiotic ointment such as Polysporin (no prescription needed). Then cover it with a Band-Aid or dressing. Change daily.
2. **Liquid Skin Bandage for Minor Cuts and Scrapes**
   - Liquid skin bandage is a new product that seals wounds with a plastic coating that lasts up to 1 week.
   - Liquid skin bandage has several benefits when compared with a regular bandage (eg, dressing, Band-Aid). Liquid bandage only needs to be applied once to minor cuts and scrapes. It helps stop minor bleeding. It seals the wound and may promote faster healing and lower infection rates. However, it is also more expensive.
   - After the wound is washed and dried, the liquid is applied by spray or with a swab. It dries in less than a minute. It's resistant to bathing.
   - This new product is available at your local pharmacy.
3. **Bruises**
   - Apply a cold pack or ice bag wrapped in a wet cloth to the bruise once for 20 minutes to stop the bleeding.
   - After 48 hours apply a warm, wet wash cloth for 10 minutes 3 times per day to help reabsorb the blood.
4. **Pain Medicine:** Give acetaminophen (eg, Tylenol) or ibuprofen (eg, Advil) as needed for pain relief (see dosage table in Appendix A or E).

5. **Call Your Doctor If**
   - Bleeding does not stop after using direct pressure to the cut.
   - Looks infected (pus, redness, increasing tenderness).
   - Doesn't heal within 10 days.
   - Your child becomes worse.

> **And remember, contact your doctor if your child develops any of the "Call Your Doctor" symptoms.**

Chapter 38

Immunization Reactions

Definition

- You believe your child is having a reaction to a recent immunization.
- Reactions to diphtheria, tetanus, acellular pertussis (DTaP); measles, mumps, rubella (MMR); polio; *Haemophilus influenzae* type b (Hib); hepatitis A; hepatitis B (HBV); influenza; chickenpox (varicella); pneumococcal; meningococcal; rotavirus; and human papillomavirus vaccines are covered.

Symptoms

- Most local swelling, redness, and pain at the injection site begins within 24 hours of the shot. It usually lasts 2 to 3 days, but with DTaP it can last 7 days.
- Fever with most vaccines begins within 24 hours and lasts 1 to 2 days.
- With live vaccines (MMR and chickenpox), fever and systemic reactions usually begin between 1 and 4 weeks.
- Severe allergic reactions are very rare but can occur with any vaccine.

When to Call Your Doctor

Call 911 Now (Your Child May Need an Ambulance) If
- Difficulty with breathing or swallowing
- Not moving or very weak
- Unresponsive or difficult to awaken

Call Your Doctor Now (Night or Day) If
- Your child looks or acts very sick
- Child is younger than 12 weeks with fever above 100.4°F (38.0°C) rectally (CAUTION: Do NOT give your baby any fever medicine before being seen.)
- Fever above 104°F (40°C) and not improved 2 hours after fever medicine
- High-pitched, unusual crying present longer than 1 hour
- Crying continuously for longer than 3 hours
- Redness or red streaking around the injection site begins more than 48 hours (2 days) after the shot
- Redness or red streak around the injection site becomes larger than 1 inch (2.5 cm)

Call Your Doctor Within 24 Hours (Between 9:00 am and 4:00 pm) If
- You think your child needs to be seen
- Fever present for more than 3 days
- Fever returns after gone for longer than 24 hours
- Measles vaccine rash (onset day 6 to 12) persists more than 3 days

Call Your Doctor During Weekday Office Hours If
- You have other questions or concerns
- Pain, tenderness, redness, or swelling at the injection site persists more than 3 days
- Fussiness from vaccine persists more than 3 days

Parent Care at Home If
- Normal immunization reaction and you don't think your child needs to be seen

Home Care Advice for Immunization Reactions

Treatment for Common Immunization Reactions

1. **Reassurance**
   - All of these reactions mean the vaccine is working.
   - Your child's body is producing new antibodies to protect against the real disease.
   - Most of these symptoms will only last 2 or 3 days.

2. **Local Reaction at Injection Site**
   - **Cold Pack:** For initial pain or tenderness at the injection site with any vaccine, apply a cold pack or ice in a wet washcloth to the area for 20 minutes each hour as needed.
   - **Pain Medicine:** Give acetaminophen (eg, Tylenol) or ibuprofen (eg, Advil) as needed (see dosage table in Appendix A or E).
   - **Localized Hives:** Apply 1% hydrocortisone cream (no prescription needed) once or twice.

3. **Fever**
   - Fever with most vaccines begins within 24 hours and lasts 2 to 3 days.
   - For fevers above 102°F (39°C), give acetaminophen (eg, Tylenol) (if child is older than 6 months, OK to give ibuprofen [eg, Advil]) (see dosage table in Appendix A or E).
   - **For All Fevers:** Give cold fluids. Avoid excessive clothing or blankets (bundling).

4. **General Reaction**
   - All vaccines can cause mild fussiness, irritability, and restless sleep. While this is usually because of a sore injection site, sometimes the cause is less clear.
   - Some children sleep more than usual. A decreased appetite and activity level are also common.
   - These symptoms do not need any treatment and will usually resolve in 24 to 48 hours.

5. **Call Your Doctor If**
   - Fever lasts more than 3 days.
   - Pain lasts more than 3 days.
   - Redness or swelling lasts more than 3 days.
   - Your child becomes worse.

Specific Immunization Reactions

1. **Chickenpox Vaccine**
   - Pain or swelling at the injection site for 1 to 2 days (in 19% of children).
   - Mild fever lasting 1 to 3 days begins 17 to 28 days after the vaccine (in 14%). Give acetaminophen or ibuprofen for fever above 102°F (39°C).
   - Never give aspirin for fever or pain, or within 6 weeks of receiving the vaccine (Reason: risk of Reye syndrome, a rare but serious brain disease).
   - Chickenpox-like vaccine rash (usually 2 lesions) at the injection site (in 3%).
   - Chickenpox-like vaccine rash (usually 5 lesions) scattered over the body (in 4%).
   - This mild rash begins 5 to 26 days after the vaccine and usually lasts a few days.
   - Children with these vaccine rashes can go to child care or school (Reason: for practical purposes, vaccine rashes are not contagious).
   - EXCEPTION: Avoid school if widespread, weepy lesions (Reason: probably actual chickenpox).
   - **Precaution:** If vaccine rash contains fluid, cover it with clothing or a Band-Aid.

2. **Diphtheria, tetanus, acelluar pertussis (DTaP) or DT Vaccine:**
   The following harmless reactions to DTaP can occur:
   - Pain, tenderness, swelling, or redness at the injection site (in 25% of children) and lasts for 24 to 48 hours.
   - Fever (in 25% of children) and lasts for 24 to 48 hours.
   - Mild drowsiness (30%), fretfulness (30%), or poor appetite (10%) and lasts for 24 to 48 hours.
   - A large swelling longer than 4 inches (10 cm) on the arm following the fourth or fifth dose of DTaP occurs in 5% of children. Most children can still move the leg or arm normally.
   - The large thigh or upper arm swelling resolves without treatment by day 3 (60%) to day 7 (90%). This is not an allergy and future DTaP vaccines can be given.

3. *Haemophilus influenzae* **Type b (Hib) Vaccine**
   - No serious reactions reported.
   - Sore injection site or mild fever only occurs in 1.5% of children.
4. **Hepatitis A Vaccine**
   - No serious reactions reported.
   - Sore injection occurs in 20% of children, loss of appetite in 10%, and headache in 5%.
   - Usually no fever.
   - If these symptoms occur, they usually last 1 to 2 days.
5. **Hepatitis B Virus (HBV) Vaccine**
   - No serious reactions reported.
   - Sore injection site occurs in 30% of children and mild fever in 3% of children.
   - Because fever from the vaccine is rare, any infant younger than 2 months with a fever following the HBV vaccine should be examined.
6. **Influenza (Seasonal or H1N1) Virus Vaccine**
   - Pain, tenderness, or swelling at the injection site occurs within 6 to 8 hours in 10% of children.
   - Mild fever below 103°F (39.5°C) occurs in 18% of children. Fevers mainly occur in young children.
   - **Nasal Influenza (Seasonal or H1N1) Vaccine:** Congested or runny nose, mild fever.
7. **Measles Vaccine**
   - The measles vaccine can cause a fever (10% of children) and rash (5% of children) about 6 to 12 days following the injection.
   - Mild fever below 103°F (39.5°C) in 10% and lasts 2 or 3 days.
   - The mild pink rash is mainly on the trunk and lasts 2 or 3 days.
   - No treatment is necessary. Your child is not contagious.
   - **Call Your Doctor If**
     - Rash becomes very itchy.
     - Rash changes to purple spots.
     - Rash lasts more than 3 days.

8. **Meningococcal Vaccine**
    - No serious reactions.
    - Sore injection site for 1 to 2 days occurs in 50% of children, with limited use of the arm in 15%. Mild fever occurs in 4%, headache in 40%, and joint pain in 20%.
    - The vaccine never causes meningitis.
9. **Mumps or Rubella Vaccine:** There are no reactions except for an occasional sore injection site.
10. **Papillomavirus Vaccine**
    - No serious reactions reported
    - Sore injection site for few days in 80% of children
    - Mild redness and swelling at the injection site (in 25%)
    - Fever above 100.4°F (38.0°C) in 10% and fever above 102°F (39°C) in 1% to 2%
11. **Pneumococcal Vaccine**
    - No serious reactions
    - Pain, tenderness, swelling, OR redness at the injection site in 15% to 30% of children
    - Mild fever below 102°F (39°C) in 15% for 1 to 2 days
12. **Polio Vaccine**
    - Polio vaccine by injection occasionally causes some muscle soreness.
    - Oral vaccine is no longer used in the United States.
13. **Rotavirus Vaccine**
    - No serious reactions to this oral vaccine
    - Mild diarrhea or vomiting for 1 to 2 days in 3%
    - No fever

> **And remember, contact your doctor if your child develops any of the "Call Your Doctor" symptoms.**

Chapter 39

Puncture Wound

Definition

- The skin is punctured by a narrow, pointed object.

Causes
- Commonly caused by a nail, sewing needle, pencil, or toothpick.
- Pencil lead is actually graphite (harmless), not poisonous lead. Even colored leads are not toxic.

See More Appropriate Topic (Instead of This One) If
- Animal caused it (see Chapter 45, Animal or Human Bite)
- Skin is cut or scraped (not punctured) (see Chapter 37, Cuts, Scrapes, or Bruises [Skin Injury])
- Foreign body (eg, sliver) remains in the skin (see Chapter 41, Skin, Foreign Body [Splinters])

When to Call Your Doctor

Call 911 Now (Your Child May Need an Ambulance) If

- Puncture on the head, neck, chest, or abdomen that may go deep

Call Your Doctor Now (Night or Day) If

- You think your child has a serious injury
- Bleeding that won't stop after 10 minutes of direct pressure
- Puncture on the head, neck, chest, or abdomen that isn't deep
- Puncture overlying a joint
- Tip of the object is broken off and missing
- Feels like something still in the wound
- Child won't stand (bear weight or walk) on punctured foot
- Needlestick from used or discarded injection needle
- Sharp object or setting was very dirty (eg, barnyard)
- No previous tetanus shots
- Dirt (debris) or pencil lead pigment is not gone after 15 minutes of scrubbing
- Severe pain
- Wound looks infected (redness, red streaks, swollen, tenderness)
- Fever occurs

Call Your Doctor Within 24 Hours (Between 9:00 am and 4:00 pm) If

- You think your child needs to be seen
- Last tetanus shot was more than 5 years ago

Call Your Doctor During Weekday Office Hours If

- You have other questions or concerns

Parent Care at Home If

- Minor puncture wound and you don't think your child needs to be seen

Home Care Advice for Puncture Wound

1. **Cleansing**
   - Wash the wound with soap and warm water for 15 minutes.
   - For any dirt or debris, scrub the wound surface back and forth with a washcloth to remove it.
   - If the wound re-bleeds a little, that may help remove germs.
2. **Trimming:** Cut off any flaps of loose skin that seal the wound and interfere with drainage or removing debris. Use a fine scissors after cleaning them with rubbing alcohol.
3. **Antibiotic Ointment:** Apply an antibiotic ointment such as Polysporin (no prescription needed). Then cover with a Band-Aid to reduce the risk of infection. Rewash the area and reapply an antibiotic ointment every 12 hours for 2 days.
4. **Pain Medicine:** Give acetaminophen (eg, Tylenol) or ibuprofen (eg, Advil) as needed for pain relief (see dosage table in Appendix A or E).
5. **Expected Course:** Puncture wounds seal over in 1 to 2 hours. Pain should resolve within 2 days.
6. **Call Your Doctor If**
   - Dirt in the wound persists after 15 minutes of scrubbing.
   - Pain becomes severe.
   - It begins to look infected (redness, red streaks, tenderness, pus, fever).
   - Your child becomes worse.

> **And remember, contact your doctor if your child develops any of the "Call Your Doctor" symptoms.**

Chapter 40

Rash or Redness, Localized and Cause Unknown

Definition

- Rash on one small part of the body (localized or clustered)
- Red or pink rash
- Small spots, large spots, or solid red
- Includes localized areas of redness or skin irritation

Causes
- **Main Cause:** Skin contact with some irritant

Return to School
- Children with localized rashes do not need to miss any child care or school.

See More Appropriate Topic (Instead of This One) If
- Insect bite (see Chapter 47, Insect Bite)

When to Call Your Doctor

Call 911 Now (Your Child May Need an Ambulance) If

- Not moving or too weak to stand

Call Your Doctor Now (Night or Day) If

- Your child looks or acts very sick
- Purple or blood-colored spots or dots that are not from injury or friction
- Bright red area or red streak (but not sunburn)
- Rash area is very painful
- Child is younger than 1 month and tiny water blisters (like chickenpox)

Call Your Doctor Within 24 Hours (Between 9:00 am and 4:00 pm) If

- You think your child needs to be seen
- Severe itching or fever is present
- Looks like a boil, infected sore, or other infected rash
- Teenager with genital area rash
- Lyme disease suspected (bull's-eye rash, tick bite or exposure)

Call Your Doctor During Weekday Office Hours If

- You have other questions or concerns
- Blisters unexplained (EXCEPTION: poison ivy)
- Pimples (apply antibiotic ointment until seen)
- Peeling fingers
- Rash lasts longer than 7 days

Parent Care at Home If

- Mild localized rash and you don't think your child needs to be seen

Home Care Advice for Localized Rashes

1. **Reassurance:** New localized rashes are usually caused by skin contact with an irritating substance.
2. **Avoid the Cause**
   - Try to find the cause.
   - Consider irritants like a plant (eg, poison ivy), chemicals (eg, solvents, insecticides), fiberglass, detergents, a new cosmetic, or new jewelry (eg, nickel).
   - A pet may be the intermediary (eg, with poison ivy or oak) or your child may react directly to pet saliva.
3. **Avoid Soap:** Wash the area once thoroughly with soap to remove any remaining irritants. Thereafter avoid soaps to this area. Cleanse the area when needed with warm water.
4. **Local Cold:** Apply a cold, wet washcloth or soak in cold water for 20 minutes every 3 to 4 hours to reduce itching or pain.
5. **Steroid Cream:** If the itch is more than mild, apply 1% hydrocortisone cream (no prescription needed) 4 times per day (EXCEPTION: suspected ringworm).
6. **Avoid Scratching:** Encourage your child not to scratch. Cut the fingernails short.
7. **Contagiousness:** Children with localized rashes do not need to miss any child care or school.
8. **Expected Course:** Most of these rashes pass in 2 to 3 days.
9. **Call Your Doctor If**
   - Rash spreads or becomes worse.
   - Rash lasts more than 1 week.
   - Your child becomes worse.

> **And remember, contact your doctor if your child develops any of the "Call Your Doctor" symptoms.**

Chapter 41

Skin, Foreign Body (Splinters)

Definition

- A foreign body (FB) (eg, splinter, fishhook, sliver of glass) is embedded in the skin.

Symptoms of a Foreign Body in the Skin
- **Pain:** Most tiny slivers (eg, cactus spine) in the superficial skin do not cause much pain. Deeper or perpendicular FBs are usually painful to pressure. FBs in the foot are very painful with weight bearing.
- **FB Sensation:** Older children may report the sensation of something being in the skin ("I feel something there").

Types of Foreign Bodies
- **Wood/Organic FBs:** Splinters, cactus spines, thorns, toothpicks.
- **Metallic FBs:** Bullets, BBs, nails, sewing needles, pins, tacks.
- Fiberglass spicules.
- Fishhooks: May have a barbed point that makes removal difficult.
- Glass.
- Pencil lead (graphite).
- Plastic FBs.

When to Call Your Doctor

Call Your Doctor Now (Night or Day) If
- Deeply embedded FB (eg, needle or toothpick in foot)
- FB has a barb (eg, fishhook)
- FB is a BB
- FB is causing severe pain
- You are reluctant to take out FB
- You can't remove FB
- Site of sliver removal looks infected (redness, red streaks, swollen, pus)
- Fever occurs

Call Your Doctor Within 24 Hours (Between 9:00 am and 4:00 pm) If
- You think your child needs to be seen
- Deep puncture wound and last tetanus shot was more than 5 years ago

Call Your Doctor During Weekday Office Hours If
- You have other questions or concerns

Parent Care at Home If
- Tiny, superficial, pain-free slivers that don't need removal
- Tiny plant stickers, cactus spines, or fiberglass spicules that need removal
- Minor sliver, splinter, or thorn that needs removal and you think you can remove it

Home Care Advice for Minor Slivers

1. **Tiny, Pain-Free Slivers:** If superficial slivers are numerous, tiny, and pain free, they can be left in. Eventually they will work their way out with normal shedding of the skin, or the body will reject them by forming a little pimple that will drain on its own.

2. **Tiny Painful Plant Stickers:** Plant stickers (eg, stinging nettle), cactus spines, or fiberglass spicules are difficult to remove because they are fragile. Usually they break when pressure is applied with tweezers.

   - **Tape:** First try to remove the small spines or spicules by touching the area lightly with packaging tape, duct tape, or another very sticky tape. If that doesn't work, try wax hair remover.
   - **Wax Hair Remover:** If tape doesn't work, apply a layer of wax hair remover. Let it air-dry for 5 minutes or accelerate the process with a hair dryer. Then peel it off with the spicules. Most will be removed. The others will usually work themselves out with normal shedding of the skin.

3. **Needle and Tweezers:** For large slivers or thorns, remove with a needle and tweezers.

   - Check the tweezers beforehand to be certain the ends (pickups) meet exactly (if they do not, bend them). Sterilize the tools with rubbing alcohol.
   - Cleanse the skin surrounding the sliver briefly with rubbing alcohol before trying to remove it. If you don't have any, use soap and water but don't soak the area if FB is wood (Reason: can cause swelling of the splinter).
   - Use the needle to completely expose the large end of the sliver. Use good lighting. A magnifying glass may help.
   - Then grasp the end firmly with the tweezers and pull it out at the same angle that it went in. Getting a good grip the first time is especially important with slivers that go in perpendicular to the skin or those trapped under the fingernail.
   - For slivers under a fingernail, sometimes a wedge of the nail must be cut away with fine scissors to expose the end of the sliver.

- Superficial horizontal slivers (where you can see all of it) usually can be removed by pulling on the end. If the end breaks off, open the skin with a sterile needle along the length of the sliver and flick it out.

4. **Antibiotic Ointment:** Wash the area with soap and water before and after removal. To reduce the risk of infection, apply an antibiotic ointment such as Polysporin (no prescription needed) once after removal.

5. **Call Your Doctor If**
   - You can't get it all out.
   - Removed but pain becomes worse.
   - Starts to look infected.
   - Your child becomes worse.

> **And remember, contact your doctor if your child develops any of the "Call Your Doctor" symptoms.**

Part 11

Skin, Widespread
Symptoms

Chapter 42

Hives

Definition

- An itchy rash made up of raised pink spots with pale centers

Symptoms
- Raised pink bumps with pale centers (welts).
- Hives look like mosquito bites.
- Sizes of hives vary from ½ inch (12 mm) to several inches (cm) across.
- Shapes of hives are variable and change repeatedly.
- Itchy rash.

Causes
- **Widespread** hives usually are caused by a viral infection. They can also be an allergic reaction to a food, a drug, an infection, an insect bite, or other substances. Often the cause is not found. Hives from foods usually resolve in 6 hours.
- **Localized** hives are usually caused by skin contact with plants, pollen, food, or pet saliva. Localized hives are not caused by drugs, infections, or swallowed foods.

See More Appropriate Topic (Instead of This One) If
- Doesn't look like hives (see Chapter 43, Rash, Widespread and Cause Unknown)
- Mosquito bites suspected (see Chapter 47, Insect Bite)

When to Call Your Doctor

Call 911 Now (Your Child May Need an Ambulance) If

- Difficulty breathing or wheezing
- Hoarseness or cough with rapid onset
- Difficulty swallowing, drooling, or slurred speech with rapid onset
- Severe life-threatening allergic reaction in the past to similar substance

Call Your Doctor Now (Night or Day) If

- Your child looks or acts very sick
- Hives began after a bee sting, medicine, or high-risk food (eg, peanuts, fish), and no previous reactions
- Child younger than 1 year with widespread hives

Call Your Doctor Within 24 Hours (Between 9:00 am and 4:00 pm) If

- You think your child needs to be seen
- Severe hives (eg, eyes swollen shut, very itchy) not improved after second dose of Benadryl
- Fever or joint swelling is present
- Abdominal pain or vomiting is present

Call Your Doctor During Weekday Office Hours If

- You have other questions or concerns
- Hives interfere with school or normal activities after taking Benadryl every 6 hours for more than 24 hours
- Food suspected as cause
- Hives have occurred 3 or more times and cause is unknown
- Hives last more than 1 week

Parent Care at Home If

- Hives with no complications and you don't think your child needs to be seen

Home Care Advice for Hives

1. **Localized Hives**
   - For localized hives, wash the allergic substance off the skin with soap and water.
   - If itchy, massage the area with a cold pack or ice for 20 minutes.
   - Localized hives usually disappear in a few hours and don't need Benadryl.

2. **Benadryl for Widespread Hives**
   - Give Benadryl 4 times per day for widespread hives that itch (no prescription needed) (see dosage table in Appendix D).
   - If you only have another antihistamine at home (but not Benadryl), use that.
   - Continue Benadryl 4 times per day until the hives are gone for 12 hours.
   - **Contraindication:** Child is younger than 1 year (Reason: Benadryl is a sedative). Give your doctor a call for advice.

3. **Food-Related Hives**
   - Foods can cause widespread hives.
   - Sometimes hives are isolated to just around the mouth.
   - Hives from foods usually are transient and gone in less than 6 hours.

4. **Cool Bath:** Give a cool bath for 10 minutes to relieve itching (CAUTION: Avoid causing a chill). Rub very itchy areas with an ice cube for 10 minutes.

5. **Remove Allergens:** Give a bath or shower if triggered by pollens or animal contact. Change clothes.

6. **Avoid Allergens:** If you identify a substance that causes hives (eg, a food), help your child avoid that substance in the future.

7. **Contagiousness**
   - Hives are not contagious.
   - Your child can return to child care or school if the hives do not interfere with normal activities.
   - If the hives are associated with an infection, your child can return to school after the fever is gone and your child feels well enough to participate in normal activities.

8. **Expected Course:** Hives from a viral illness normally come and go for 3 or 4 days, then disappear. Most children get hives once.

9. **Call Your Doctor If**
   - Severe hives persist after second dose of Benadryl.
   - Most of the itch is not relieved within 24 hours on continuous Benadryl.
   - Hives last more than 1 week.
   - Your child becomes worse.

And remember, contact your doctor if your child develops any of the "Call Your Doctor" symptoms.

Chapter 43

Rash, Widespread and Cause Unknown

Definition

- Rash over large areas or most of the body (widespread or generalized)
- Occasionally just on hands, feet, and buttocks—but both sides of body
- Red or pink rash
- Small spots, large spots, or solid red skin

Causes
- **Main Cause:** A 2- or 3-day rash occurring with a viral illness. Viral rashes usually have symmetrical pink spots on the trunk.

Return to School
- Most viral rashes are no longer contagious once the fever is gone.
- For minor rashes, your child can return to child care or school after the FEVER is gone.
- For major rashes, your child can return to child care or school after the RASH is gone or your doctor says it's safe to return with the rash.

See More Appropriate Topic (Instead of This One) If
- Hives (especially if itchy) (see Chapter 42, Hives)
- Sunburn (see Chapter 44, Sunburn)
- Measles vaccine rash (fine pink rash occurring 7 to 10 days after measles vaccine) (see Chapter 38, Immunization Reactions)

When to Call Your Doctor

Call 911 Now (Your Child May Need an Ambulance) If

- Purple or blood-colored rash with fever
- Sudden onset of rash (within 2 hours) and also has difficulty with breathing or swallowing
- Not moving or too weak to stand

Call Your Doctor Now (Night or Day) If

- Your child looks or acts very sick
- Purple or blood-colored rash WITHOUT fever
- Bright red skin that peels off in sheets
- Large blisters on skin
- Bloody crusts on lips
- Taken a prescription medication within the last 3 days
- Fever
- Menstruating and using tampons

Call Your Doctor Within 24 Hours (Between 9:00 am and 4:00 pm) If

- Widespread rash but none of the symptoms described herein (Reason: needs a diagnosis)

Home Care Advice for Widespread Rashes
(Pending Talking With Your Doctor)

1. **For Non-Itchy Rashes:** No treatment is necessary except for heat rashes, which respond to cool baths.
2. **For Itchy Rashes**
   - Wash the skin once with soap to remove irritants.
   - Then give your child cool baths without any soap 4 times per day for 10 minutes whenever the itch is uncomfortable (CAUTION: Avoid any chill).
   - Follow with calamine lotion or a baking soda solution (1 teaspoon in 4 oz of water or 5 mL in 120 mL of water).
3. **Fever Medicine:** For fever above 102°F (39°C), give acetaminophen (eg, Tylenol) or ibuprofen (eg, Advil) (see dosage table in Appendix A or E).
4. **Contagiousness**
   - If your child has a fever, avoid contact with other children and especially pregnant women until a diagnosis is made.
   - Most viral rashes are contagious (especially if a fever is present).
   - Your child can return to child care or school after the rash is gone or your doctor says it's safe to return with the rash.
5. **Expected Course:** Most viral rashes disappear within 48 hours.
6. **Call Your Doctor If**
   - Your child becomes worse.

> **And remember, contact your doctor if your child develops any of the "Call Your Doctor" symptoms.**

Chapter 44

Sunburn

Definition

- Red or blistered skin from sun overexposure.
- The pain and swelling starts at 4 hours, peaks at 24 hours, and improves after 48 hours.

Severity of Sunburn
- Most sunburn is a first-degree burn that turns the skin pink or red.
- Prolonged sun exposure can cause blistering and a second-degree burn.
- Sunburn never causes a third-degree burn or scarring.

When to Call Your Doctor

Call 911 Now (Your Child May Need an Ambulance) If

- Passed out or too weak to stand

Call Your Doctor Now (Night or Day) If

- Your child looks or acts very sick
- Fever above 104°F (40°C)
- Unable to look at lights because of eye pain
- Extremely painful sunburn
- Looks infected (eg, draining pus, red streaks, increasing tenderness after day 2)

Call Your Doctor Within 24 Hours (Between 9:00 am and 4:00 pm) If

- You think your child needs to be seen
- Large blisters (bigger than ½ inch or 12 mm)
- Many small blisters
- Swollen feet interfere with walking
- Blisters on the face

Call Your Doctor During Weekday Office Hours If

- You have other questions or concerns

Parent Care at Home If

- Mild sunburn and you don't think your child needs to be seen

Home Care Advice for Mild Sunburn

Treating Mild Sunburn

1. **Ibuprofen:** Start ibuprofen (eg, Advil, Motrin) for pain relief as soon as possible (ASAP) if child is older than 6 months (Reason: if this anti-inflammatory agent is begun within 6 hours of sun exposure and continued for 2 days, it can reduce the swelling and discomfort experienced).

2. **Steroid Cream**
   - Apply 1% hydrocortisone cream as soon as possible 3 times per day (no prescription needed).
   - If used early and continued for 2 days, it may reduce swelling and pain.
   - Use a moisturizing cream until you can get some.

3. **Cool Baths**
   - Apply cool compresses to the burned area several times a day to reduce pain and burning.
   - For larger sunburns, give cool baths for 10 minutes (CAUTION: Avoid any chill). Add 2 oz (60 mL) baking soda per tub.
   - Avoid soap on the sunburn.

4. **Extra Fluids:** Offer extra water on the first day to replace the fluids lost into the sunburn and to prevent dehydration and dizziness.

5. **Blisters**
   - CAUTION: Leave closed blisters alone (Reason: to prevent infection).
   - For broken blisters, trim off the dead skin with a fine scissors cleaned with rubbing alcohol.

6. **Antibiotic Ointment**
   - For any large, open blisters, apply an antibiotic ointment such as Polysporin (no prescription needed). Remove it with warm water and reapply it twice a day for 3 days.

7. **Expected Course:** Pain usually stops after 2 or 3 days. Peeling usually occurs on day 5 to 7.

8. **Call Your Doctor If**
   - Pain becomes severe.
   - Sunburn looks infected.
   - Your child becomes worse.

Preventing Sunburn

1. **Sunscreens:** Use a sunscreen with an SPF of 15 or higher. Fair-skinned children (with red or blond hair) need a sunscreen with an SPF of 30.
   - Apply sunscreen 30 minutes before exposure to the sun to give it time to penetrate the skin. Give special attention to the areas most likely to become sunburned, such as the nose, ears, cheeks, and shoulders.
   - Reapply sunscreen every 3 to 4 hours, as well as after swimming or profuse sweating. A "waterproof" sunscreen stays on for about 30 minutes in water.
   - Most people apply too little sunscreen. The average adult requires 1 oz of sunscreen per application.
   - The best way to prevent skin cancer is to prevent sunburns.

2. **Infants and Sunscreens**
   - The skin of infants is thinner than the skin of older children and more sensitive to the sun. Therefore, try to keep babies younger than 6 months in the shade and out of direct sunlight. If they have to be in the sun, use sunscreens, longer clothing, and a hat with a brim.
   - When a sunscreen is needed, infants can use adult sunscreens (American Academy of Pediatrics recommendation) even though the Food and Drug Administration hasn't approved their use for children younger than 6 months. There are no reported harmful side effects from today's sunscreens.

3. **Protect Lips, Nose, and Eyes**
   - To prevent sunburned lips, apply a lip coating that contains sunscreen.
   - If the nose or some other area has been repeatedly burned during the summer, protect it completely from all the sun's rays with zinc oxide or titanium oxide ointment.
   - Protect your child's eyes from the sun's rays and cataracts with good sunglasses.

4. **High-Risk Children**
   - If your child has red or blond hair, has fair skin, and never tans, she is at increased risk for sunburn.
   - These children need to use a sunscreen even for brief exposures.
   - They should avoid sun exposure whenever possible.
5. **Time of Day:** Avoid exposure to the sun during the hours of 10:00 am to 3:00 pm, when the sun's rays are most intense (CAUTION: When overcast, more than 70% of the sun's rays still get through the clouds).

And remember, contact your doctor if your child develops any of the "Call Your Doctor" symptoms.

Part 12

Bites or Stings

Chapter 45

Animal or Human Bite

Definition

- Bite or claw wound from a pet, farm, or wild animal
- Bite from a human child or adult

Risk of Bites

- Animal or human bites usually need to be seen because all of them are contaminated with saliva and prone to wound infection.

Types of Wounds

- **Bruising:** There is no break in the skin. There is no risk of infection.
- **Scrape (Abrasion) or Scratch:** A superficial wound that doesn't go all the way through the skin. There is low risk of infection. Preventive antibiotics are not indicated.
- **Laceration (Cut):** A wound that goes through the skin (dermis) to the fat or muscle tissue. There is an intermediate risk of infection. Most need to be seen. Wound cleansing and irrigation can help prevent infection by washing out the bacteria from the wound. Preventive antibiotics may be required.
- **Puncture Wound:** There is an intermediate risk of infection. Puncture wounds from cat bites are especially prone to getting infected; many physicians will prescribe preventive antibiotics for cat bites.

Types of Bites

- **Bites From Rabies-Prone Wild Animals:** Rabies is a fatal disease. Bites or scratches from a bat, skunk, raccoon, fox, coyote, or large wild animal are especially dangerous. These animals can transmit rabies even if they have no symptoms. In the United States, 90% of cases of rabies in humans are attributed to bats. Bats have transmitted rabies without a detectable bite mark.

- **Small Wild Animal Bites:** Rodents such as mice, rats, moles, gophers, chipmunks, prairie dogs, and rabbits fortunately are considered free of rabies. Squirrels rarely carry rabies but have not transmitted it to humans.
- **Large Pet Animal Bites:** Most bites from pets are from dogs or cats. Bites from domestic animals such as horses can be handled using these guidelines. Dogs and cats are free of rabies in most metro areas. Stray animals are always at risk for rabies until proven otherwise. Cats and dogs that are never allowed to roam freely outdoors are considered free of rabies. The main risk in pet bites is serious wound infection, not rabies. Cat bites become infected more often than dog bites. Claw wounds from cats are treated the same as bite wounds because the claws may be contaminated with saliva.
- **Small Indoor Pet Animal Bites:** Small indoor pets (eg, gerbils, hamsters, guinea pigs, white mice) are at no risk for rabies. Tiny puncture wounds from these small animals also don't need to be seen. They carry a small risk for wound infections.
- **Human Bites:** Most human bites occur during fights, especially in teenagers. Sometimes a fist is cut when it strikes a tooth. Human bites are more likely to become infected than animal bites. Bites on the hands are at increased risk of complications. Many toddler bites are safe because they don't break the skin.

Dogs and Cats and the Risk of Rabies

- **Indoor Versus Outdoor Pets:** Dogs and cats that are never allowed to roam freely outdoors are considered free of rabies. Outdoor pets who are stray, sick, or unvaccinated AND living in communities where rabies occurs in pets are considered at risk for rabies in the United States and Canada.
- **Metropolitan Versus Rural Location:** Dogs and cats in most metropolitan areas in the United States and Canada are free of rabies (EXCEPTION: towns along the border with Mexico). Dogs and cats in rural areas have a higher risk of rabies.

- **Provoked Versus Unprovoked Bite:** An unprovoked attack by a domestic animal increases the likelihood that an animal is rabid. Note that bites inflicted while a person is attempting to feed or handle a healthy animal are considered provoked.
- **Developing Countries Versus United States and Canada:** Dogs and cats in developing countries have a higher risk of rabies; rabies postexposure prophylaxis is indicated if a bite occurs in a developing country. International travelers need to remain alert.
- Nurses and physicians must check with the local public health department about the risk for rabies in their community.

First Aid Advice for Bleeding: Apply direct pressure to the entire wound with a clean cloth.

First Aid Advice for All Bites and Scratches: Wash all bite wounds and scratches immediately with soap and warm water.

When to Call Your Doctor

Call 911 Now (Your Child May Need an Ambulance) If
- Major bleeding that can't be stopped (see First Aid Advice)
- Not moving or too weak to stand

Call Your Doctor Now (Night or Day) If
- Your child looks or acts very sick
- Bleeding won't stop with 10 minutes of direct pressure (continue pressure until seen)
- Any contact with an animal at risk for RABIES
- Wild animal bite that breaks the skin
- Pet animal (eg, dog, cat) bite that breaks the skin (EXCEPTION: bruise or superficial scratches that don't go through the skin or tiny puncture wound)
- Puncture wound (holes through skin) from CAT teeth or claws
- Puncture wound of hand or face
- Human bite that breaks the skin
- Bite looks infected (redness or red streaks) or fever
- Bat contact or exposure, even without a bite mark
- See First Aid Advice for all new bites

Call Your Doctor Within 24 Hours (Between 9:00 am and 4:00 pm) If
- You think your child needs to be seen
- Last tetanus shot was more than 5 years ago

Call Your Doctor During Weekday Office Hours If
- You have other questions or concerns

Parent Care at Home If
- **Pet Animal Bite:** Tiny puncture wound or superficial scratches (EXCEPTION: cat puncture wound)
- Any bite that didn't break the skin (bruise)

Home Care Advice for Animal or Human Bite

1. **Cleansing**
   - Wash all wounds immediately with soap and water for 5 minutes.
   - Also flush vigorously under running water for a few minutes (Reason: can prevent many wound infections).
   - Scrub the wound enough to make it re-bleed a little (Reason: helps with cleaning out the wound).

2. **Bleeding:** For any bleeding, apply continuous pressure for 10 minutes.

3. **Antibiotic Ointment:** For small cuts, apply an antibiotic ointment (eg, Polysporin, Bacitracin) to the bite 3 times a day for 3 days (no prescription needed).

4. **Pain Medicine:** Give acetaminophen (eg, Tylenol) or ibuprofen (eg, Advil) as needed for pain relief (see dosage table in Appendix A or E).

5. **Bruises:** Apply a cold pack or ice bag wrapped in a wet washcloth once for 20 minutes (Reason: reduce bleeding, pain, and swelling).

6. **Expected Course:** Most scratches, scrapes, and other minor bites heal up fine in 5 to 7 days.

7. **Call Your Doctor If**
   - Wound begins to look infected (pus, redness, red streaks).
   - Fever occurs.
   - Your child becomes worse.

And remember, contact your doctor if your child develops any of the "Call Your Doctor" symptoms.

Chapter 46

Bee or Yellow Jacket Sting

Definition

- Your child was stung by a honeybee, bumblebee, hornet, paper wasp, or yellow jacket.
- More than 95% of stings are from honeybees or yellow jackets.

Local Reactions
- The sting involves injecting venom into the human from the bee's stinger.
- The main symptoms are pain, itching, swelling, and redness at the sting site.
- Severe pain or burning at the site lasts 1 to 2 hours. Itching often follows the pain.
- **Swelling:** Normal swelling from venom can increase for 24 hours following the sting. Stings of the upper face can cause severe swelling around the eye, but this is harmless.
- **Redness:** Bee stings can normally become red. That doesn't mean they are infected. Infections rarely occur in stings.
- The redness can last 3 days and the swelling 7 days.

Anaphylactic Reaction
- A severe life-threatening allergic reaction is called anaphylaxis.
- The main symptoms are difficulty breathing and swallowing starting within 2 hours of the sting.
- Anaphylactic reactions to bee stings occur in 4 out of 1,000 children.
- The onset of widespread hives or facial swelling alone following a bee sting is usually an isolated symptom, not the forerunner of anaphylaxis. Your child's doctor will decide.

See More Appropriate Topic (Instead of This One) If

- Not a bee, wasp, or yellow jacket sting (see Chapter 47, Insect Bite)

First Aid Advice for Anaphylaxis—Epinephrine (Pending Emergency Medical Services Arrival)

- If you have epinephrine (EpiPen or Twinject), give it now.
- Do this while calling 911 (Reason: life-saving advice).
- **Dose if Your Child Weighs More Than 66 Pounds (30 kg):** 0.3 mg. Auto-inject EpiPen or give 0.3 mL Twinject.
- **Dose if Your Child Weighs Between 33 and 66 Pounds (15 to 30 kg):** 0.15 mg. Auto-inject EpiPen Jr or give 0.15 mL Twinject.
- **Dose if Your Child Weighs Less Than 33 Pounds (15 kg):** Give dosage recommended by your doctor (or 0.1 mL if you have an epinephrine ampule).
- Inject it into the muscle (intramuscular or IM) of the upper outer thigh.
- Can be given through clothing if necessary.
- **Benadryl:** After giving epinephrine, give oral Benadryl or other antihistamine, if your child is able to swallow.

First Aid Advice for Anaphylactic Shock: Lie down with the feet elevated.

When to Call Your Doctor

Call 911 Now (Your Child May Need an Ambulance) If

- For any of the following symptoms of anaphylaxis, see First Aid Advice. Anaphylaxis usually starts within 20 minutes and always by 2 hours following a sting.
- Wheezing or difficulty breathing
- Hoarseness, cough, or tightness in the throat or chest
- Difficulty swallowing or drooling
- Speech is confused or slurred
- Passed out or very weak
- Previous severe allergic reaction to bees or yellow jackets (not just hives)

Call Your Doctor Now (Night or Day) If

- Your child looks or acts very sick
- Hives or swelling occur elsewhere on the body
- Sting inside the mouth
- Sting to the eye
- Abdominal pain or vomiting
- More than 5 stings per 10 pounds (5 kg) of weight (for teens, more than 50 stings)

Call Your Doctor Within 24 Hours (Between 9:00 am and 4:00 pm) If

- You think your child needs to be seen
- Sting looks infected (red streaking from the sting area, yellow drainage) (Note: infection and cellulitis don't start until at least 24 to 48 hours after the sting. Any redness starting in the first 24 hours is caused by venom.)
- Swelling is huge (eg, spreads beyond a joint such as the wrist or ankle)

Call Your Doctor During Weekday Office Hours If

- You have other questions or concerns

Parent Care at Home If

- Normal local reaction to yellow jacket or bee sting and you don't think your child needs to be seen

Home Care Advice for Bee or Yellow Jacket Sting

1. **Try to Remove the Stinger (if Present)**
   - Only honeybees leave a stinger.
   - Use a fingernail or credit card edge to scrape it off.
   - If the stinger is below the skin surface, leave it alone. It will be shed with normal skin healing.

2. **Meat Tenderizer**
   - Apply a meat tenderizer/water solution on a cotton ball for 20 minutes (EXCEPTION: near the eye). This may neutralize the venom and decrease pain and swelling.
   - If not available, apply aluminum-based deodorant or a baking soda solution for 20 minutes.

3. **Local Cold:** For persistent pain, massage with an ice cube for 10 minutes.

4. **Pain Medicine:** Give acetaminophen (eg, Tylenol) or ibuprofen (eg, Advil) immediately for relief of pain and burning (see dosage table in Appendix A or E).

5. **Antihistamine:** If the sting becomes itchy, give a dose of Benadryl (see dosage table in Appendix D).

6. **Hydrocortisone Cream:** For itching or swelling, apply 1% hydrocortisone cream to the sting area 3 times per day (no prescription needed).

7. **Expected Course:** Severe pain or burning at the site lasts 1 to 2 hours. Normal swelling from venom can increase for 24 hours following the sting. The redness can last 3 days and the swelling 7 days.

8. **Call Your Doctor If**
   - Your child develops difficulty breathing or swallowing (mainly during the 2 hours after the sting) **(call 911).**
   - Redness lasts more than 3 days.
   - Swelling becomes huge or spreads beyond the wrist or ankle.
   - Sting begins to look infected.
   - Your child becomes worse.

And remember, contact your doctor if your child develops any of the "Call Your Doctor" symptoms.

Chapter 47

Insect Bite

Definition

- Child was bitten by an insect (bug).
- Most are mosquito bites.
- This chapter excludes bees, ticks, and spiders.

Symptoms

- Insect bites usually cause a small red bump.
- Often it looks like localized hives (one large bump or several small ones).
- Sometimes a small water blister occurs in the center of the bump, especially in younger children.
- **Itchy Insect Bites:** Bites of mosquitoes, chiggers (harvest mites), fleas, and bedbugs usually cause itchy, red bumps.
- **Painful Insect Bites:** Bites of horseflies, deer flies, gnats, fire ants, harvester ants, blister beetles, and centipedes usually cause a painful, red bump. Within a few hours, fire ant bites can change to blisters or pimples.

Mosquito Bites: Types of Reactions

- In North America, mosquito bites are usually just an annoyance, causing very itchy red skin bumps. Often it looks like localized hives (one large bump or several small ones).
- When a mosquito bites an individual, various chemicals are injected into the skin. The red bumps are actually the body's allergic reaction to these chemicals. The skin reaction can look like a hive.
- Suspect mosquito bites if there are bites on other parts of the body. Mosquito bites of the upper face can cause the eyelid to swell up for several days. With bites, the swelling can be pink as well as large (especially in children aged 1 to 5 years).
- However, the mosquito can sometimes be a carrier of blood-borne diseases (eg, West Nile virus).

Anaphylaxis

- A severe life-threatening allergic reaction is called anaphylaxis.
- The main symptoms are difficulty breathing and swallowing starting within 2 hours of the sting. Onset usually is within 20 minutes.
- Anaphylaxis can occur with bee, yellow jacket, wasp, or fire ant stings. Anaphylactic reactions are very rare following other insect bites.

See More Appropriate Topic (Instead of This One) If

- Bee or yellow jacket sting (see Chapter 46, Bee or Yellow Jacket Sting)
- Tick bite (see Chapter 48, Tick Bite)
- Doesn't look like an insect bite (see Chapter 40, Rash or Redness, Localized and Cause Unknown)

First Aid Advice for Anaphylaxis—Epinephrine (Pending Emergency Medical Services Arrival)

- If you have epinephrine (EpiPen or Twinject), give it now.
- Do this while calling 911 (Reason: life-saving advice).
- **Dose if Your Child Weighs More Than 66 Pounds (30 kg):** 0.3 mg. Auto-inject EpiPen or give 0.3 mL Twinject.
- **Dose if Your Child Weighs Between 33 and 66 Pounds (15 to 30 kg):** 0.15 mg. Auto-inject EpiPen Jr or give 0.15 mL Twinject.
- **Dose if Your Child Weighs Less Than 33 Pounds (15 kg):** Give dosage recommended by your doctor (or 0.1 mL if you have an epinephrine ampule).
- Inject it into the muscle (intramuscular or IM) of the upper outer thigh.
- Can be given through clothing if necessary.
- **Benadryl:** After giving epinephrine, give oral Benadryl or other antihistamine, if your child is able to swallow.

First Aid Advice for Anaphylactic Shock: Lie down with the feet elevated.

When to Call Your Doctor

Call 911 Now (Your Child May Need an Ambulance) If

- For any of the following symptoms of anaphylaxis, see First Aid Advice. Onset usually is within 20 minutes and always by 2 hours following the bite.
- Difficulty breathing or wheezing
- Hoarseness or cough with rapid onset
- Difficulty swallowing, drooling, or slurred speech with rapid onset
- Previous severe life-threatening allergic reaction to same insect bite
- Difficult to awaken
- Confused thinking or talking

Call Your Doctor Now (Night or Day) If

- Your child looks or acts very sick
- Stiff neck (can't touch chin to chest)
- Hives or swelling elsewhere on the body
- More than 20 fire ant stings in a child younger than 1 year

Call Your Doctor Within 24 Hours (Between 9:00 am and 4:00 pm) If

- You think your child needs to be seen
- Severe pain is not improved 2 hours after pain medicine given
- New redness or red streak around the bite begins more than 48 hours (2 days) after the bite
- Redness or red streak around the bite becomes larger than 1 inch

Call Your Doctor During Weekday Office Hours If

- You have other questions or concerns
- Scab that looks infected (drains pus or increases in size) not improved after applying antibiotic ointment for 2 days

Parent Care at Home If

- Normal insect bite and you don't think your child needs to be seen
- You have questions about insect repellents (eg, DEET)

Home Care Advice for Insect Bites

Treatment for Insect Bites

1. **Reassurance**
   - Most insect bites result in a red bump. Some are larger (like a hive). Some have a small water blister in the center. These are normal reactions to an insect bite.
   - A large hive at the bite site does not mean your child has an allergy.
   - The redness does not mean the bite is infected.

2. **Itchy Insect Bites (Including All Mosquito Bites)**
   - **Steroid Cream:** To reduce the itching, use 1% hydrocortisone cream (no prescription needed). Apply 4 times a day until the itch is gone. If not available, apply a baking soda paste until you can get some.
   - If neither is available, apply an ice cube in a wet washcloth for 20 minutes.
   - Also apply firm, sharp, direct, steady pressure to the bite for 10 seconds to reduce the itch. A fingernail, pen cap, or other object can be used.
   - **Antihistamine:** If the bite is very itchy after local treatment, try an oral antihistamine such as Benadryl (no prescription needed) (see dosage table in Appendix D). Sometimes it helps, especially in allergic children.

3. **Painful Insect Bites**
   - Rub the bite for 15 to 20 minutes with a cotton ball soaked in a baking soda solution once. This will usually reduce the pain.
   - You can also apply an ice cube in a wet washcloth for 20 minutes. Give acetaminophen (eg, Tylenol) or ibuprofen (eg, Advil) as needed for pain relief (see dosage table in Appendix A or E).
   - Antihistamines don't help.

4. **Antibiotic Ointment**
   - If the insect bite has a scab on it and the scab looks infected, apply an antibiotic ointment such as Polysporin 3 times per day (no prescription needed).
   - Cover the scab with a Band-Aid to prevent scratching and spread.
   - Repeat washing the sore, applying antibiotic ointment, and covering with a Band-Aid 3 times per day until healed.

- CAUTION: For spreading infections (redness or red streaks), your child needs to be seen.
5. **Expected Course**
   - Most insect bites are itchy for several days.
   - Any pinkness or redness usually lasts 3 days.
   - Swelling may last 7 days.
   - Insect bites of the upper face can cause severe swelling around the eye, but this is harmless.
   - Swelling is usually worse in the morning after lying down all night. It will improve after standing for a few hours.
6. **Call Your Doctor If**
   - Severe pain persists longer than 2 hours after pain medicine.
   - Infected scab doesn't improve after 48 hours of antibiotic ointment.
   - Bite looks infected (new redness starts after 48 hours).
   - Your child becomes worse.

Prevention of Insect Bites

1. **Prevention**
   - Wear long pants, long-sleeved shirts, and a hat.
   - Avoid being outside when the insect is most active. Many insects that cause itchy bites are most active at sunrise or sunset (eg, chiggers, no-see-ums, mosquitoes).
   - Insect repellents containing DEET are effective in preventing many insect bites. Read the label carefully.
2. **DEET Products:** Apply to skin.
   - DEET is a very effective mosquito repellent. It also repels ticks and other bugs.
   - The American Academy of Pediatrics (2003) has approved the use of DEET in a concentration of 30% or less for all children older than 2 months. Use 30% DEET if you need 6 hours of protection. Use 10% DEET if you only need protection for 2 hours.
   - Don't apply DEET to the hands if the child sucks on her thumbs or fingers (Reason: prevent ingestion).
   - Warn older children who apply their own repellent that a total of 3 or 4 drops can protect the whole body.

- Apply to exposed areas of skin. Do not apply to eyes or mouth. Do not apply to skin that is covered by clothing. Don't put any repellent on areas that are sunburned or have rashes because DEET is more easily absorbed in these areas.
- Remember to wash it off with soap and water when your child returns indoors.
- CAUTION: DEET can damage clothing made of synthetic fibers, plastics (eg, eyeglasses), and leather. DEET can be applied to cotton clothing.

3. **Permethrin Products**
   - Apply to clothing.
   - Permethrin-containing products (eg, Duranon, Permanone) are highly effective mosquito repellents. They also repel ticks.
   - An advantage over using DEET is that they are applied to clothing instead of skin.
   - Apply it to shirt cuffs, pant cuffs, shoes, and hats.
   - You can also put it on other outdoor items (eg, shoes, mosquito screens, sleeping bags).
   - Do not apply permethrin to skin, as it will lose effectiveness very quickly.

4. **Picaridin Products**
   - Picaridin is a newly approved repellent that is equivalent to 10% DEET.
   - It can safely be applied to skin or clothing.

And remember, contact your doctor if your child develops any of the "Call Your Doctor" symptoms.

Chapter 48

Tick Bite

Definition

- A tick (small brown bug) is attached to the skin.
- A tick recently was removed from the skin.

Symptoms
- The bite is painless and doesn't itch, so ticks may go unnoticed for a few days.
- After feeding on blood, ticks become quite swollen and easy to see.
- Ticks eventually fall off on their own after sucking blood for 3 to 6 days.

Causes
- The wood tick (dog tick) is the size of a watermelon seed and can sometimes transmit Rocky Mountain spotted fever and Colorado tick fever.
- The deer tick is between the size of a poppy seed (pinhead) and an apple seed, and can sometimes transmit Lyme disease.

Lyme Disease
- The risk of Lyme disease following a recognized deer tick bite in a high-risk area is estimated to be only 1.4%.
- Almost all infections start with a bull's-eye rash (erythema migrans) at the site of the tick bite.
- Antibiotics can be given at this time.
- The routine use of antibiotics following tick bites to prevent Lyme disease is not recommended.

See More Appropriate Topic (Instead of This One) If
- Not a tick bite (see Chapter 47, Insect Bite)

When to Call Your Doctor

Call Your Doctor Now (Night or Day) If

- Your child looks or acts very sick
- You can't remove the tick after trying the advice in this chapter
- You can't remove tick's head that broke off in the skin after trying the advice in this chapter (Note: if the removed tick is moving, it was completely removed.)
- Widespread rash occurs 2 to 14 days following the bite
- Fever or severe headache occurs 2 to 14 days following the bite
- Bite looks infected (red streaking from the bite area, yellow drainage) (Note: infection doesn't start until at least 24 to 48 hours after the bite.)

Call Your Doctor Within 24 Hours (Between 9:00 am and 4:00 pm) If

- You think your child needs to be seen
- Red-ring or bull's-eye rash occurs around a deer tick bite (Lyme disease rash begins 3 to 30 days after the bite)
- Weak, droopy face or crooked smile

Call Your Doctor During Weekday Office Hours If

- You have other questions or concerns

Parent Care at Home If

- Tick bite with no complications and you don't think your child needs to be seen

Home Care Advice for Tick Bites

Treating Tick Bites

1. **Reassurance**
   - Most tick bites are harmless.
   - The spread of disease by ticks is rare.
   - If the tick is still attached to the skin, it will need to be removed.
   - Covering the tick with petroleum jelly, nail polish, or rubbing alcohol doesn't work. Neither does touching the tick with a hot or cold object.
   - Try one of the following techniques:

2. **Wood Tick Removal: Try Soapy Cotton Ball First**
   - Apply liquid soap to a cotton ball until it's soaked.
   - Cover the tick with the soap-soaked cotton ball.
   - Let it stay on the tick for 30 seconds.
   - The tick will usually be stuck to the cotton ball when you lift it away.

3. **Wood Tick Removal: Try Tweezers Second**
   - Use tweezers and grasp the tick close to the skin (on its head).
   - Pull the wood tick straight upward without twisting or crushing it.
   - Maintain a steady pressure until it releases its grip.
   - If tweezers aren't available, use fingers, a loop of thread around the jaws, or a needle between the jaws for traction.

4. **Deer Tick Removal:** Tiny deer ticks need to be scraped off with a fingernail or credit card edge.

5. **Tick's Head**
   - If the wood tick's head breaks off in the skin, remove it.
   - Clean the skin with rubbing alcohol.
   - Use a sterile needle to uncover the head and lift it out.
   - If a small piece of the head remains, the skin will eventually shed it.
   - If most of the head is left, call your doctor.

6. **Antibiotic Ointment:** Wash the wound and your hands with soap and water after removal to prevent catching any tick disease. Apply antibiotic ointment such as Polysporin to the bite once (no prescription needed).

7. **Expected Course:** Tick bites normally don't itch or hurt. That's why they often go unnoticed.

8. **Call Your Doctor If**
   - You can't remove the tick or the tick's head.
   - Fever or rash in the next 2 weeks.
   - Bite begins to look infected.
   - Your child becomes worse.

Preventing Tick Bites

1. **Prevention**
   - When hiking in tick-infested areas, wear long clothing and tuck the ends of pants into socks. Apply an insect repellent to shoes and socks.
   - Permethrin products applied to clothing are more effective than DEET products against ticks.

2. **Tick Repellent for Skin: DEET**
   - DEET is an effective tick repellent.
   - Use 30% DEET for children and adolescents (American Academy of Pediatrics recommendation, 2003) (30% DEET protects for 6 hours).

3. **Tick Repellent for Clothing: Permethrin**
   - Permethrin-containing products (eg, Duranon, Permanone) are highly effective tick repellents.
   - An advantage over using DEET is that they are applied to and left on clothing instead of skin. Apply it to clothes, especially pants cuffs, socks, and shoes. You can also put it on other outdoor items (eg, mosquito screen, sleeping bags).
   - Do not apply permethrin to skin (Reason: it's rapidly degraded on contact with skin).

And remember, contact your doctor if your child develops any of the "Call Your Doctor" symptoms.

Part 13

Fever
Symptoms

Chapter 49

Fever

Definition

- Your child has a fever if
  - **Rectal, Ear, or Temporal Artery (TA) Temperature:**
    100.4°F (38.0°C) or higher.
  - **Oral or Pacifier Temperature:** 100°F (37.8°C) or higher.
  - **Under the Arm (Axillary or Armpit) Temperature:**
    99°F (37.2°C) or higher.
  - **Limitation:** Ear (tympanic membrane) temperatures are not
    reliable before 6 months of age.
  - Temporal artery and skin infrared temperatures may be reliable
    in young infants.
  - Use this guideline if fever is your child's only symptom.

Causes

- **Main Cause:** Colds and other viral infections.
- Fever may be the only symptom for the first 24 hours (ie, viral
  fevers). The onset of symptoms (eg, runny nose, cough, diarrhea)
  are often delayed. In the case of roseola, fever may be the only
  symptom for 2 or 3 days.
- The cause of fever usually can't be determined until other
  symptoms develop. That may take 24 hours.
- Bacterial infections (eg, strep throat, urinary tract infections)
  also cause fever.
- Teething does not cause fever.

Fever and Crying

- Fever on its own shouldn't cause much crying.
- Frequent crying in a child with fever is caused by pain until proven
  otherwise.
- Possible causes are ear infections, urinary tract infections, and sore throats.

Normal Variation of Temperature

- **Rectal:** A reading of 98.6°F (37°C) is just the average rectal temperature. It normally can change from 96.8°F (36°C) in the morning to a high of 100.3°F (37.9°C) in the late afternoon.
- **Oral:** A reading of 97.6°F (36.5°C) is just the average oral temperature. It normally can change from a low of 95.8°F (35.5°C) in the morning to a high of 99.9°F (37.7°C) in the late afternoon.

Return to School

- Your child can return to child care or school after the fever is gone and your child feels well enough to participate in normal activities.

See More Appropriate Topic (Instead of This One) If

- Other symptom is present with the fever—see that chapter (eg, Chapter 11, Colds; Chapter 23, Cough; Chapter 19, Sore Throat; Chapter 9, Earache; Chapter 14, Sinus Pain or Congestion; Chapter 28, Diarrhea; Chapter 29, Vomitting With Diarrhea; Chapter 30, Vomiting Without Diarrhea; Chapter 43, Rash, Widespread and Cause Unknown)
- Fever onset within 24 hours of receiving vaccine (see Chapter 38, Immunization Reactions)
- Fever onset 6 to 12 days after measles vaccine OR 17 to 28 days after chickenpox vaccine (see Chapter 38, Immunization Reactions)

When to Call Your Doctor

Call 911 Now (Your Child May Need an Ambulance) If
- Not moving or very weak
- Unresponsive or difficult to awaken
- Difficulty breathing with bluish lips
- Purple or blood-colored spots or dots on skin

Call Your Doctor Now (Night or Day) If
- Your child looks or acts very sick
- Not alert when awake
- Any difficulty breathing
- Great difficulty swallowing fluids or saliva
- Child is confused (delirious) or has stiff neck or bulging soft spot
- Had a seizure with the fever
- Child is younger than 12 weeks with fever above 100.4°F (38.0°C) rectally (CAUTION: Do not give your baby any fever medicine before being seen.)
- Fever above 104°F (40°C) and not improved 2 hours after fever medicine
- Very irritable (eg, inconsolable crying, cries when touched or moved)
- Won't move an arm or leg normally
- Signs of dehydration (eg, very dry mouth, no urine in more than 8 hours)
- Burning or pain with urination
- Pain suspected
- Chronic disease (eg, sickle cell disease) or medication (eg, chemotherapy) that causes decreased immunity

Call Your Doctor Within 24 Hours (Between 9:00 am and 4:00 pm) If
- You think your child needs to be seen
- Child 3 to 6 months of age with fever
- Child 6 to 24 months of age with fever present longer than 24 hours but no other symptoms (ie, no cold, cough, diarrhea, etc)
- Fever repeatedly above 104°F (40°C) despite fever medicine
- Fever returns after gone for longer than 24 hours
- Fever present for more than 3 days

Call Your Doctor During Weekday Office Hours If

- You have other questions or concerns

Parent Care at Home If

- Fever with no other symptoms and you don't think your child needs to be seen

Home Care Advice for Fever

1. **Reassurance:** Presence of a fever means your child has an infection, usually caused by a virus. Most fevers are good for sick children and help the body fight infection. Use the following definitions to help put your child's level of fever into perspective:
   - 100°F to 102°F (37.8°C to 39°C): **Low-Grade Fevers:** Beneficial, desirable range.
   - 102°F to 104°F (39°C to 40°C): **Average Fever:** Beneficial.
   - Above 104°F (40°C): **High Fever:** Causes discomfort but harmless.
   - Above 106°F (41.1°C): **Very High Fever:** Important to bring it down.
   - Above 108°F (42.3°C): **Dangerous Fever:** Fever itself can cause brain damage.

2. **Treatment for All Fevers: Extra Fluids and Less Clothing**
   - Give cold fluids orally in unlimited amounts (Reason: good hydration replaces sweat and improves heat loss from the skin).
   - Dress in 1 layer of lightweight clothing and sleep with 1 light blanket (avoid bundling) (CAUTION: Overheated infants can't undress themselves).
   - For fevers 100°F to 102°F (37.8°C to 39°C), this is the only treatment needed (fever medicines are unnecessary).

3. **Fever Medicine**
   - Fevers only need to be treated with medicine if they cause discomfort. That usually means fevers above 102°F (39°C).
   - Give acetaminophen (eg, Tylenol) or ibuprofen (eg, Advil) (see dosage table in Appendix A or E).
   - The goal of fever therapy is to bring the temperature down to a comfortable level. Remember, fever medicine usually lowers the fever by 2°F to 3°F (1°C to 1.5° C).

- Avoid aspirin (Reason: risk of Reye syndrome, a rare but serious brain disease).
- Avoid alternating acetaminophen and ibuprofen (Reason: unnecessary and risk of overdosage).

4. **Sponging**
   - Note: sponging is optional for high fevers, not required.
   - **Indication:** May sponge if fever above 104°F (40°C) doesn't come down with acetaminophen (eg, Tylenol) or ibuprofen (eg, Advil) (always give fever medicine first).
   - **How to Sponge:** Use lukewarm water (85°F to 90°F) (29.4°C to 32.2°C). Do not use rubbing alcohol. Sponge for 20 to 30 minutes.
   - If your child shivers or becomes cold, stop sponging or increase the water temperature.

5. **Contagiousness:** Your child can return to child care or school after the fever is gone and your child feels well enough to participate in normal activities.

6. **Expected Course of Fever:** Most fevers associated with viral illnesses fluctuate between 101°F and 104°F (38.4°C and 40°C) and last for 2 or 3 days.

7. **Call Your Doctor If**
   - Fever rises above 104°F (40°C) repeatedly.
   - Any fever occurs if your child is younger than 12 weeks.
   - Fever without a cause persists longer than 24 hours (if your child is younger than 2 years).
   - Fever persists more than 3 days (72 hours).
   - Your child becomes worse.

And remember, contact your doctor if your child develops any of the "Call Your Doctor" symptoms.

Chapter 50

Fever: Myths Versus Facts

Misconceptions about fever are commonplace. Many parents needlessly worry and lose sleep when their child has a fever. This is called fever phobia. Overall, fevers are harmless. Let the following facts help you put fever into perspective:

. . . .

Myth: My child feels warm, so she has a fever.

Fact: Children can feel warm for many reasons such as playing hard, crying, getting out of a warm bed, or being outside on a hot day. They are "giving off heat." Their skin temperature should return to normal in 10 to 20 minutes. Once these causes are excluded, about 80% of children who feel warm and act sick actually have a fever. If you want to be sure, take your child's temperature. The following are the cutoffs for fever using different types of thermometers:

- **Rectal, Ear, or Temporal Artery Thermometers:**
  100.4°F (38.0°C) or higher
- **Oral or Pacifier Thermometers:**
  100°F (37.8°C) or higher
- **Under the Arm (Axillary or Armpit) Thermometers:**
  99°F (37.2°C) or higher

. . . .

Myth: All fevers are bad for children.

Fact: Fevers turn on the body's immune system and help the body fight infection. Fevers are one of the body's protective mechanisms. Normal fevers between 100°F and 104°F (37.8°C and 40°C) are actually good for sick children.

. . . .

Myth: Fevers above 104°F (40°C) are dangerous and can cause brain damage.

Fact: Fevers with infections don't cause brain damage. Only body temperatures above 108°F (42.3°C) can cause brain damage. The body temperature climbs this high only with extreme environmental temperatures (eg, if a child is confined to a closed car in hot weather).

Myth: Anyone can have a febrile seizure (seizure triggered by fever).

Fact: Only 4% of children can have a febrile seizure.

Myth: Febrile seizures are harmful.

Fact: Febrile seizures are scary to watch, but they usually stop within 5 minutes. They cause no permanent harm. Children who have had febrile seizures do not have a greater risk for developmental delays, learning disabilities, or seizures without fever.

Myth: All fevers need to be treated with fever medicine.

Fact: Fevers only need to be treated if they cause discomfort. Usually fevers don't cause any discomfort until they go above 102°F or 103°F (39°C or 39.5°C).

Myth: Without treatment, fevers will keep going higher.

Fact: Wrong. Because the brain has a thermostat, fevers from infection usually don't go above 103°F or 104°F (39.5°C or 40°C). They rarely go to 105°F or 106°F (40.6°C or 41.1°C). While the latter are "high" fevers, they are harmless ones.

Myth: With treatment, fevers should come down to normal.

Fact: With treatment, fevers usually come down 2°F or 3°F (1°C or 1.5°C).

. . . .

Myth: If the fever doesn't come down (ie, if you can't "break the fever"), the cause is serious.

Fact: Fevers that don't respond to fever medicine can be caused by viruses or bacteria. It doesn't relate to the seriousness of the infection.

. . . .

Myth: Once the fever comes down with medicines, it should stay down.

Fact: The fever will normally last for 2 or 3 days with most viral infections. Therefore, when fever medicine wears off, the fever will return and need to be treated again. Fever will go away and not return once your child's body overpowers the virus (usually by the fourth day).

. . . .

Myth: If the fever is high, the cause is serious.

Fact: If the fever is high, the cause may or may not be serious. If your child looks very sick, the cause is more likely to be serious.

. . . .

Myth: The exact number of the temperature is very important.

Fact: How your child looks is what's important, not the exact temperature.

. . . .

Myth: Oral temperatures between 98.7°F and 100°F (37.1°C and 37.8°C) are low-grade fevers.

Fact: These temperatures are normal variations. The body's temperature normally changes throughout the day. It peaks in the late afternoon and evening. An actual low-grade fever is 100°F to 102°F (37.8°C to 39°C).

. . . .

Summary: Remember that fever is fighting off your child's infection. Fever is one of the good guys.

Chapter 51

Fever: How to Take a Temperature

Definition of Fever

- **Rectal, Ear, or Temporal Artery (TA) Temperature:** 100.4°F (38.0°C) or higher.
- **Oral or Pacifier Temperature:** 100°F (37.8°C) or higher.
- **Under the Arm (Axillary or Armpit) Temperature:** 99°F (37.2°C) or higher.
- **Limitation:** Ear (tympanic membrane) temperatures are not reliable before 6 months of age.

Where to Take a Temperature

- Temperatures measured rectally are the most accurate. Temperatures measured orally, by electronic pacifier, or by ear canal or TA are also accurate if done properly. Temperatures measured in the armpit are the least accurate, but they are better than no measurement.
- **Child Younger Than 3 Months (90 Days):** An armpit temperature is the safest and may be preferred for screening. If the armpit temperature is above 99°F (37.2°C), check the rectal temperature. The reason you need to take a rectal temperature for young infants is that if they have a true fever, they need to be evaluated immediately by a doctor.
- **Child Younger Than 4 or 5 Years:** A rectal or electronic pacifier temperature is reliable. An ear or TA thermometer can be used after 6 months of age. An axillary (armpit) temperature is adequate for screening if it is taken correctly.
- **Child Older Than 4 or 5 Years:** Take the temperature orally (by mouth), by ear thermometer, or by TA thermometer.

How to Take a Rectal Temperature

• Have your child lie stomach down on your lap.
• Put some petroleum jelly on the end of the thermometer and on the opening of the anus.
• Slide the thermometer gently into the opening of the anus for about 1 inch. If your child is younger than 6 months, put it in only about ½ inch (inserting until the silver tip disappears is about ½ inch).
• Hold your child still and leave the thermometer in for about 20 seconds with a digital electronic thermometer. (Note: the AAP recommends that older glass thermometers be discarded because they contain mercury. If that's all you have, however, leave it in for about 2 minutes to get an accurate reading.)
• Your child has a fever if the rectal temperature is above 100.4°F (38°C).

How to Take an Armpit Temperature

• Put the tip of the thermometer in an armpit. Make sure the armpit is dry.
• Close the armpit by holding the elbow against the chest for 4 or 5 minutes. The tip of the thermometer must be covered by skin.
• Your child has a fever if the armpit temperature is above 99°F (37.2°C). If you have any doubt, take your child's temperature rectally.

How to Take an Oral Temperature

• Be sure your child has not had a cold or hot drink in the last 30 minutes.
• Put the tip of the thermometer under one side of the tongue and toward the back. It's important to put it in the right place.
• Have your child hold the thermometer in place with her lips and fingers (not teeth) for about 30 seconds with a digital electronic thermometer. (Note: the AAP recommends that older glass thermometers be discarded because they contain mercury. If that's all you have, however, leave it in for about 3 minutes to get an accurate reading.) Keep the lips sealed.
• Your child has a fever if the temperature is above 100°F (37.8°C).

How to Take a Digital Electronic Pacifier Temperature

- Have your child suck on the pacifier until it reaches a steady state and you hear a beep.
- This usually takes 3 to 4 minutes.
- Your child has a fever if the pacifier temperature is above 100°F (37.8°C).

How to Take an Ear Temperature

- This thermometer reads the infrared heat waves released by the eardrum.
- An accurate temperature depends on pulling the ear backward to straighten the ear canal (back and up if your child is older than 1 year).
- Then aim the tip of the ear probe midway between the opposite eye and earlobe.
- The biggest advantage of this thermometer is that it measures temperatures in less than 2 seconds. It also does not require cooperation by the child and does not cause any discomfort.
- **Limitation:** If your child has been outdoors on a cold day, he needs to be inside for 15 minutes before taking his temperature. Earwax, ear infections, and ear tubes, however, do not interfere with accurate readings.

How to Take a Temporal Artery Temperature

- The thermometer reads the infrared heat waves released by the TA, which runs across the forehead just below the skin.
- Place the sensor head at the center of the forehead midway between the eyebrow and hairline.
- To scan for your child's temperature, depress the scan button and keep it depressed.
- Slowly slide the TA thermometer straight across the forehead toward the top of the ear, keeping in contact with the skin.
- Stop when you reach the hairline and release the scan button.
- Remove the thermometer from the skin and read your child's temperature on the display screen.

Part 14

Miscellaneous

Chapter 52

Antibiotics: When Do They Help?

Definition

Antibiotics are strong medicines that can kill bacteria. Antibiotics have saved many lives and prevented bacterial complications. However, antibiotics do not kill viruses. One of the decisions health care professionals make every day is whether a child's infection is viral or bacterial. Consider their perspective.

Bacterial Infections: Antibiotics Can Help and Will Be Prescribed

Bacterial infections are much less common than viral infections. Bacteria cause

- Most ear infections (but they only happen to 5% of children with a cold)
- Most sinus infections (but they only happen to 5% of children with a cold)
- 20% of sore throats (strep throat infections)
- 10% of pneumonia (bacterial lung infection)

Viral Infections: Antibiotics Do NOT Help

Viruses cause most infections in children, including

- Colds present for less than 2 weeks, unless they turn into an ear or sinus infection
- Coughs present for less than 3 weeks, unless they develop bacterial pneumonia
- 95% of fevers
- 80% of sore throats
- 90% of pneumonia (Most pneumonia in children is viral.)
- 99% of diarrhea and vomiting

Cold Symptoms That Are Confusing But Normal

These symptoms are sometimes mistaken as signs of bacterial infections and a reason for starting antibiotics.

- **Green or Yellow Nasal Discharge:** This is usually a normal part of recovery from a cold, rather than a clue to a sinus infection.
- **Green or Yellow Phlegm (Sputum):** This is a normal part of viral bronchitis, not a sign of pneumonia.
- **High Fevers:** A high fever (above 104°F or 40°C) can be caused by a virus or bacteria.

Side Effects of Antibiotics

All antibiotics have side effects. Unless your child really needs an antibiotic, there is no reason to risk side effects of the medicine. Some children taking antibiotics develop diarrhea, nausea, vomiting, or a rash. Diarrhea usually occurs because the antibiotic has killed off healthy intestinal bacteria. And if your child gets a rash, your doctor must decide if the rash is an allergic reaction to the drug or not. The biggest side effect of overuse is increasing resistance to antibiotics.

Giving Antibiotics for Viral Infections: What Happens?

If your child has a viral illness, an antibiotic will not shorten the course of fever or help other symptoms. Antibiotics will not get your child back to school or you back to work sooner. If your child develops side effects from the antibiotic, he will feel worse instead of better.

What You Can Do

- Save antibiotics for diagnosed bacterial infections when your child really needs them.
- Don't pressure your child's doctor for a prescription for an antibiotic.
- Treat your child's cold and cough symptoms with home remedies that work.
- Remember that fever is fighting the infection and producing antibodies to prevent future viral infections.

Chapter 53

Coughs and Colds: Medicines or Home Remedies?

Medicines

Over-the-counter (OTC) cough and cold medicines can cause serious side effects in young children. The risks of using these medicines outweigh any benefits from reducing symptoms. Therefore, in October 2008, the Food and Drug Administration recommended that OTC cough and cold medicines never be used in children younger than 4 years. From ages 4 to 6 years, they should be used only if recommended by your child's doctor. After age 6 years, the medicines are safe to use, but follow the dosage instructions on the package. Fortunately, you can easily treat coughs and colds in young children without these nonprescription medicines.

Home Remedies

A good home remedy is safe, inexpensive, and as beneficial as OTC medicines. They are also found in nearly every home. Here is how you can treat your child's symptoms with simple but effective home remedies instead of medicines.

1. **Runny Nose:** Just suction or blow it. And remember, when your child's nose runs like a faucet, it's getting rid of viruses. Antihistamines (eg, Benadryl) do not help the average cold. However, they are useful and approved if the runny nose is caused by nasal allergies (hay fever).
2. **Blocked Nose:** Use nasal washes.
   - Use saline nose spray or drops to loosen up dried mucus, followed by blowing or suctioning the nose. If these are not available, warm water will work fine.
   - Instill 2 to 3 drops in each nostril. Do one side at a time. Then suction or blow. Teens can just splash warm water into their nose. Repeat nasal washes until the return is clear.

- Do nasal washes whenever your child can't breathe through the nose. For infants on a bottle or breast, use nose drops before feedings.
- Saline nose drops and sprays are available in all pharmacies without a prescription. To make your own, add ½ teaspoon (2 mL) of table salt to 1 cup (8 oz or 240 mL) of warm tap water.
- **Sticky, Stubborn Mucus:** Remove with a wet cotton swab.
- **Medicines:** There is no medicine that can remove dried mucus or pus from the nose.

3. **Coughing:** Use homemade cough medicines.
   - **For Children 3 Months to 1 Year of Age:** Give warm, clear fluids (eg, warm water, apple juice). Dosage is 1 to 3 teaspoons (5 to 15 mL) 4 times per day when coughing. Avoid honey because it can cause infantile botulism. If your child is younger than 3 months, see your child's doctor.
   - **For Children 1 Year and Older:** Use HONEY, ½ to 1 teaspoon (2 to 5 mL), as needed. It thins secretions and loosens the cough. (If honey is not available, you can use corn syrup.) Recent research has shown that honey is better than drugstore cough syrups at reducing the frequency and severity of nighttime coughing.
   - **For Children 6 Years and Older:** Use COUGH DROPS to coat the irritated throat. (If cough drops are not available, you can use hard candy.)
   - **Coughing Spasms:** Expose your child to warm mist from a shower.

4. **Fluids:** Help your child drink plenty of fluids. Staying well hydrated thins the body's secretions, making it easier to cough and blow the nose.

5. **Humidity:** If the air in your home is dry, use a humidifier. Moist air keeps nasal mucus from drying up and lubricates the airway. Running a warm shower for a while can also help humidify the air.

Treatment Is Not Always Needed

- If symptoms aren't bothering your child, they don't need medicine or home remedies. Many children with a cough or nasal congestion are happy, play normally, and sleep peacefully.
- Only treat symptoms if they cause discomfort, interrupt sleep, or really bother your child (eg, a hacking cough).
- Because fevers are beneficial, only treat them if they slow your child down or cause some discomfort. That doesn't usually occur until your child's temperature reaches 102°F (39°C) or higher. Acetaminophen (eg, Tylenol) or ibuprofen (eg, Advil, Motrin) can be safely used in these instances to treat fever or pain (see dosage table in Appendix A or E for indications and age limitations).

Summary: If treatment is needed for coughs and colds, home remedies may work better than medicines.

Chapter 54

Emergency Symptoms Not to Miss

You would not overlook or underestimate the seriousness of major bleeding, not breathing, severe choking, a seizure, or a coma (can't wake up). These are life-threatening emergencies and you would rightfully call 911. For poisoning, you would call 1-800-222-1222. Some emergency symptoms, however, are difficult to recognize or not always considered serious. If your child has any of the following symptoms, call your child's doctor immediately or go to the nearest emergency department.

- **Sick newborn**
  Your baby is younger than 1 month and looks sick (eg, vomiting, cough, poor color) or acts abnormal (eg, poor feeding, excessive sleeping) in any way. At this age, these symptoms are serious until proven otherwise. During the first month of life, infections can progress quickly.
- **Severe lethargy**
  Your child stares into space, won't smile, won't play at all, or hardly responds to you. Your child is too weak to cry, floppy, or hard to awaken. These are serious symptoms. Note: sleeping more when sick is normal, but when awake your child should be alert.
- **Confusion**
  The sudden onset of confusion (delirium). Your child is awake but says strange things, sees things, and doesn't recognize you. Note: transient delirium can be seen for 5 minutes or so with higher fevers. However, if not brief, confusion can have some serious causes.

- **Severe pain**
  Severe pain is incapacitating. It interferes with all normal activities.
  The child just wants to be left alone. If your child cries when you
  try to hold or move him, this can be a symptom of meningitis or
  appendicitis. Children also are unable to sleep or can only fall
  asleep briefly.

- **Inconsolable crying**
  Inconsolable, constant crying is caused by severe pain until proven
  otherwise. Suspect this in children who are unable to sleep or will
  only fall asleep briefly, and when awake will not engage in any
  normal activities. CAUTION: Instead of constant crying, severe
  pain may cause your child to groan, moan, or whimper.

- **Can't walk**
  If your child has learned to walk and then loses the ability to stand
  or walk, she may have a serious injury to the legs or a problem with
  balance. If your child walks bent over, holding her belly, she may
  have a serious problem such as appendicitis.

- **Tender abdomen**
  Press on your child's belly while he is sitting on your lap and looking
  at a book. You should be able to press an inch or so in with your
  fingers in all parts of the belly without a problem. If your child winces
  or screams, it suggests a serious cause. If the belly is bloated and hard
  along with the pain, the problem is even more worrisome. Note: if
  your child just pushes your hand away, it probably means you
  haven't distracted him enough.

- **Tender testicle or scrotum**
  Sudden pain in the groin area can be from twisting (torsion) of the
  testicle. This requires surgery within 8 hours to save the testicle.

- **Hard time breathing**
  Breathing is essential for life. Most childhood deaths are due to
  severe breathing problems. If your child has trouble breathing,
  tight croup (harsh sound when breathing in called stridor), or
  obvious wheezing or grunting with each breath, she needs to be
  seen immediately. Other signs of respiratory distress are fast
  breathing, bluish lips, or retractions (skin pulling in between the
  ribs). Children with severe respiratory distress can't drink, talk,

or cry. Note: nasal congestion causes vibrations and some noisy breathing but usually without any trouble breathing. Check breathing after you clean out the nose with nasal washes and suction.

- **Bluish lips**
Bluish lips, tongue, or gums (cyanosis) can mean a reduced amount of oxygen in the bloodstream. Note: blueness only present around the mouth (but not the lips) can be caused by being cold.

- **Drooling**
The sudden onset of drooling or spitting when your child is ill means your child is having trouble swallowing. The cause can be a serious infection of the tonsils, throat, or epiglottis (top part of the windpipe). A serious allergic reaction can also cause trouble swallowing. Swelling in the throat could close off the airway.

- **Dehydration**
Dehydration means that your child's body fluids are low. Dehydration usually follows severe vomiting or diarrhea. Suspect dehydration if your child has not urinated in 8 hours (more than 12 hours if your child is older than 1 year), crying produces no tears, the inside of the mouth is dry rather than moist, or the soft spot in the skull is sunken. Dehydrated children are also tired and weak. If your child is alert and active but not making much urine, she is not yet dehydrated. Children with severe dehydration become dizzy when they stand. Dehydration requires immediate fluid replacement by mouth or vein.

- **Bulging soft spot**
The soft spot in your baby's head is tense and bulging. This means the brain is under pressure.

- **Stiff neck**
To test for a stiff neck, lay your child down, then lift his head until his chin touches the middle of his chest. If he is resistant, place a toy or other object of interest on the belly so he will have to look down to see it. Older children can simply be asked to look at their belly button. A stiff neck can be an early sign of meningitis.

- **Injured neck**
Talk to your child's doctor about any neck injury, regardless of the symptoms. Neck injuries carry a risk of damage to the spinal cord.

- **Purple or blood-red spots or dots**
  Unexplained purple or blood-red spots or dots on the skin could be
  a sign of a serious bloodstream infection, especially if your child also
  has a fever. Note: bumps and bruises on the shins from active play
  are different.
- **Any fever (above 100.4°F or 38°C) in the first 3 months of life**
  Bacterial infections in young infants can cause serious complications.
  All children younger than 3 months with a fever need to be examined
  as soon as possible to determine if the cause is viral or bacterial.
- **Fever above 105°F (40.6°C)**
  All the preceding symptoms are stronger indicators of serious illness
  than the level of fever. All of them can occur with low-grade fevers
  as well as high ones. Fevers alone are considered a risk factor for
  serious infections only when the child's temperature rises above
  105°F (40.6°C). Therefore if your child has a fever above 104°F
  (40°C) that doesn't come down below 104°F after taking a fever
  medicine, call your child's doctor.
- **Chronic diseases**
  Most active chronic diseases can have some complications.
  If your child has a chronic disease, be sure to find out what those
  complications are and how to recognize them. Chronic diseases
  at highest risk for serious infections are those that weaken the
  immune system (eg, sickle cell disease, HIV, chemotherapy, organ
  transplant, chronic steroids). If you are talking with a doctor or
  nurse who doesn't normally see your child, always tell the doctor
  or nurse about your child's chronic disease (eg, asthma). Never
  assume the doctor or nurse already knows this.

Chapter 55

Infection Exposure Questions: Contagiousness

- This chapter includes information about the transmission of common infections, including how long to stay out of school or child care.
- **Incubation Period:** Interval between exposure to the infection and onset of symptoms.
- **Contagious Period:** Interval during which a sick child's disease is contagious to others. With precautions, children sometimes can return to child care and school before this period is over.
- **Infections That Are Not Contagious:** Many common bacterial infections are not contagious (eg, ear infections, sinus infections, bladder infections, kidney infections, pneumonia). Sexually transmitted infections are not contagious to children unless there is sexual contact or shared bathing.

Infection Exposure Table

Disease	Incubation Period (Days)	Contagious Period (Days)
Skin Infections/Rashes		
Chickenpox	10–21	2 days before rash until all sores have crusts (6–7 days)
Fifth disease (erythema infectiosum)	4–14	7 days before rash until rash begins
Hand-foot-and-mouth disease	3–6	Onset of mouth ulcers until fever gone
Impetigo (strep or staph)	2–5	Onset of sores until 24 hours on antibiotic
Lice	7	Onset of itch until 1 treatment
Measles	8–12	4 days before rash until 4 days after rash appears
Roseola	9–10	Onset of fever until rash gone (2 days)
Rubella (German measles)	14–21	7 days before rash until 5 days after rash appears
Scabies	30–45	Onset of rash until 1 treatment
Scarlet fever	3–6	Onset of fever or rash until 24 hours on antibiotic
Shingles (contagious for chickenpox)	14–16	Onset of rash until all sores have crusts (7 days) (Note: no need to isolate if sores can be kept covered)
Warts	30–180	Minimally contagious
Respiratory Infections		
Bronchiolitis	4–6	Onset of cough until 7 days
Colds	2–5	Onset of runny nose until fever gone
Cold sores (herpes)	2–12	[a]
Coughs (viral) or croup (viral)	2–5	Onset of cough until fever gone
Diphtheria	2–5	Onset of sore throat until 4 days on antibiotic
Influenza	1–2	Onset of symptoms until fever gone longer than 24 hours
Sore throat, strep	2–5	Onset of sore throat until 24 hours on antibiotic
Sore throat, viral	2–5	Onset of sore throat until fever gone
Tuberculosis	6–24 months	Until 2 weeks on drugs (Note: Most childhood tuberculosis is not contagious.)
Whooping cough	7–10	Onset of runny nose until 5 days on antibiotic

Disease	Incubation Period (Days)	Contagious Period (Days)
Intestinal Infections		
Diarrhea, bacterial	1–5	b
Diarrhea, *Giardia*	7–28	b
Diarrhea, traveler	1–6	b
Diarrhea, viral (rotavirus)	1–3	b
Hepatitis A	14–50	2 weeks before jaundice begins until jaundice resolved (7 days)
Pinworms	21–28	Minimally contagious; staying home is unnecessary.
Vomiting, viral	2–5	Until vomiting stops
Other Infections		
Infectious mononucleosis	30–50	Onset of fever until fever gone (7 days)
Meningitis, bacterial	2–10	7 days before symptoms until 24 hours on intravenous antibiotics in hospital
Meningitis, viral	3–6	Onset of symptoms and for 1–2 weeks
Mumps	12–25	5 days before swelling until swelling gone (7 days)
Pinkeye without pus (viral)	1–5	Mild infection; staying home is unnecessary.
Pinkeye with pus (bacterial)	2–7	Onset of pus until 1 day on antibiotic eyedrops

[a]**Cold Sores:** If child is younger than 6 years, cold sores are contagious until dry (4 to 5 days). No isolation is necessary if sores are on a part of body that can be covered. If child is older than 6 years, no isolation is necessary if the child is beyond the touching, picking stage.

[b]**Diarrhea Precautions:** Diarrhea is contagious until stools are formed. Stay home until fever is gone, diarrhea is mild, blood and mucus are gone, and toilet-trained child has control over loose stools. *Shigella* and *Escherichia coli* O157 require extra precautions. Consult your child care provider about attendance restrictions.

Appendixes

Drug Dosage Tables

Appendix A

Acetaminophen (for Fever and Pain)

Child's Weight (lb)	7–13	14–20	21–27	28–41	42–55	56–83	84–111	112+	lb
Infant Drops 80 mg/0.8 mL	0.4	0.8	1.2	1.6	2.4	—	—	—	mL
Syrup 160 mg/5 mL (teaspoon)	—	½	¾	1	1½	2	3	4	tsp
Chewable 80-mg Tablets	—	—	1½	2	3	4	5–6	8	tablets
Chewable 160-mg Tablets	—	—	—	1	1½	2	3	4	tablets
Adult 325-mg Tablets	—	—	—	—	—	1	1½	2	tablets
Adult 500-mg Tablets	—	—	—	—	—	—	1	1	tablets

Indications: Treatment of fever and pain.

Table Note

- AGE LIMIT
  - Don't use if your child is younger than 12 weeks (Reason: fever during the first 12 weeks of life needs to be documented in a medical setting and if present, your infant needs a complete evaluation). EXCEPTION: fever from immunization if child is 8 weeks or older.
  - Avoid multi-ingredient products in children younger than 6 years (Reason: Food and Drug Administration recommendations, 10/2008).
- DOSAGE: Determine by finding your child's weight in the top row of the dosage table.
- BRAND NAMES: Tylenol, FeverAll (suppositories), generic acetaminophen.
- FREQUENCY: Repeat every 4 to 6 hours as needed. Don't give more than 5 times a day.
- ADULT DOSAGE: 650 mg.
- MELTAWAYS: Dissolvable tablets that come in 80 and 160 mg (junior strength).
- SUPPOSITORIES: Acetaminophen also comes in 80-, 120-, 325-, and 650-mg suppositories (the rectal dose is the same as the dosage given by mouth).
- EXTENDED RELEASE: Avoid 650-mg oral products in children (Reason: they are every-8-hour extended release).
- MEASURING THE DOSAGE: Syringes and droppers are more accurate than teaspoons. If possible, use the syringe or dropper that comes with the medication. If you use a teaspoon, it should be a measuring spoon. Regular spoons are not reliable. Also, remember that 1 level teaspoon equals 5 mL and ½ teaspoon equals 2.5 mL.

Appendix B

Chlorpheniramine (Antihistamine)

Child's Weight (lb)	22–32	33–43	44–54	55–65	66–76	77–87	88+	lb
Liquid 2 mg/5 mL (teaspoon)	½	¾	1	1	1½	1½	2	tsp
Tablets 4 mg	—	—	½	½	½	1	1	tablets

Indications: For allergic reactions, hay fever, hives, and itching.

Table Notes

• AGE LIMIT
  – For **allergies,** don't use if your child is younger than 1 year (Reason: it's a sedative).
  – For **colds,** not recommended at any age (Reason: no proven benefits) and should be avoided if your child is younger than 4 years.
  – Avoid multi-ingredient products in children younger than 6 years (Reason: Food and Drug Administration recommendations, 10/2008).
• DOSAGE: Determine by finding your child's weight in the top row of the dosage table.
• ADULT DOSAGE: 4 mg. Repeat every 6 to 8 hours as needed.
• 6 to 12 YEARS LONG-ACTING (LA) DOSAGE: 8-mg LA tablet every 12 hours as needed.
• 12 YEARS AND OLDER LA DOSAGE: 12-mg LA tablet every 12 hours as needed.
• Brompheniramine dosage is the same as chlorpheniramine dosage.
• MEASURING THE DOSAGE: Syringes and droppers are more accurate than teaspoons. If possible, use the syringe or dropper that is packaged with the medication. If you use a teaspoon, it should be a measuring spoon. Regular spoons are not reliable. Also, remember that 1 level teaspoon equals 5 mL and ½ teaspoon equals 2.5 mL.

Appendix C

Dextromethorphan (DM) (Cough Suppressant)

Child's Weight (lb)	16-31	32-47	48-63	64-79	80-95	96-129	130+	lb
Liquid 5 mg/5 mL (teaspoon)	½	1	1½	2	2½	3	—	tsp
Liquid 7.5 mg/5 mL (teaspoon)	—	—	1	1	1½	2	3	tsp
Liquid 10 mg/5 mL (teaspoon)	—	—	—	1	1	1½	2	tsp

Indications: Cough suppressant.

Table Notes

- AGE LIMIT
  - Don't use if your child is younger than 4 years (Reason: risk of overdosage).
  - **Children Older Than 4 Years:** Not recommended as primary treatment of cough. Use honey instead.
  - Avoid multi-ingredient products in children younger than 6 years (EXCEPTION: DM combined with guaifenesin) (Reason: Food and Drug Administration recommendations, 10/2008).
- DOSAGE: Determine by finding your child's weight in the top row of the dosage table. DM is present in most cough syrups.
- ADULT DOSE: 20 mg.
- FREQUENCY: Repeat every 6 to 8 hours as needed.
- MEASURING THE DOSAGE: Syringes and droppers are more accurate than teaspoons. If possible, use the syringe or dropper that comes with the medication. If you use a teaspoon, it should be a measuring spoon. Regular spoons are not reliable. Also, remember that 1 level teaspoon equals 5 mL and ½ teaspoon equals 2.5 mL.

Appendix D

Diphenhydramine (eg, Benadryl) (Antihistamine)

Child's Weight (lb)	20–24	25–37	38–49	50–99	100+	lb
Liquid 12.5 mg/5 mL (teaspoon)	¾	1	1½	2	—	tsp
Chewable 12.5-mg Tablets	—	1	1½	2	4	tablets
Tablets 25 mg	—	½	½	1	2	tablets
Capsules 25 mg	—	—	—	1	2	capsules

Indications: For allergic reactions, hay fever, hives, and itching.

Table Notes

- AGE LIMIT
  - For **allergies,** don't use if your child is younger than 1 year (Reason: it's a sedative).
  - For **colds,** not recommended at any age (Reason: no proven benefits) and should be avoided if your child is younger than 4 years.
  - Avoid multi-ingredient products in children younger than 6 years (Reason: Food and Drug Administration recommendations, 10/2008).
- DOSAGE: Determine by finding your child's weight in the top row of the dosage table.
- FREQUENCY: Repeat every 6 hours as needed.
- ADULT DOSAGE: 50 mg.
- CHILDREN'S BENADRYL FASTMELTS: Each Fastmelt tablet contains the equivalent of 12.5 mg of diphenhydramine hydrochloride and is dosed the same as chewable tablets.
- MEASURING THE DOSAGE: Syringes and droppers are more accurate than teaspoons. If possible, use the syringe or dropper that comes with the medication. If you use a teaspoon, it should be a measuring spoon. Regular spoons are not reliable. Also, remember that 1 level teaspoon equals 5 mL and ½ teaspoon equals 2.5 mL.

Appendix E

Ibuprofen (for Fever and Pain)

Child's Weight (lb)	12–17	18–23	24–35	36–47	48–59	60–71	72–95	96+	lb
Infant Drops 50 mg/1.25 mL	1.25	1.875	2.5	3.75	5	—	—	—	mL
Liquid 100 mg/5 mL (teaspoon)	½	¾	1	1½	2	2½	3	4	tsp
Chewable 50-mg Tablets	—	—	2	3	4	5	6	8	tablets
Junior-Strength 100-mg Tablets	—	—	—	—	2	2½	3	4	tablets
Adult 200-mg Tablets	—	—	—	—	1	1	1½	2	tablets

Indications: Treatment of fever and pain.

Table Notes

- **AGE LIMIT**
  - Don't use if your child is younger than 6 months (Reason: safety not established and doesn't have Food and Drug Administration [FDA] approval).
  - Avoid multi-ingredient products in children younger than 6 years (Reason: FDA recommendations, 10/2008).
- **DOSAGE:** Determine by finding your child's weight in the top row of the dosage table.
- **BRAND NAMES:** Advil, Motrin, generic ibuprofen.
- **ADULT DOSAGE:** 400 mg.
- **FREQUENCY:** Repeat every 6 to 8 hours as needed.
- **INFANT DROPS:** Ibuprofen infant drops come with a measuring syringe.
- **MEASURING THE DOSAGE:** Syringes and droppers are more accurate than teaspoons. If possible, use the syringe or dropper that comes with the medication. If you use a teaspoon, it should be a measuring spoon. Regular spoons are not reliable. Also, remember that 1 level teaspoon equals 5 mL and ½ teaspoon equals 2.5 mL.

Appendix F

Pseudoephedrine (Decongestant)

Child's Weight (lb)	18–26	27–35	36–53	54–71	72–139	140+	lb
Infant Drops 7.5 mg/0.8 mL	0.8	1.2	1.6	—	—	—	mL
Liquid 15 mg/5 mL (teaspoon)	½	¾	1	1½	2	—	tsp
Chewable 15-mg Tablets	—	—	1	1½	2	4	tablets
Tablets 30 mg	—	—	—	—	1	2	tablets
Tablets 60 mg	—	—	—	—	—	1	tablets

Indications: Treatment of nasal congestion (stuffiness).

Table Notes

- AGE LIMIT: Don't use if your child is younger than 4 years because of the following:
  - **Reason 1:** Not approved by Food and Drug Administration (FDA) because dosage not studied in this age range.
  - **Reason 2:** Risk of dosage error causing high blood pressure.
  - CAUTION: Never give 2 cough or cold medicines at the same time (Reason: may share an ingredient and cause poisoning).
  - Avoid multi-ingredient products in children younger than 6 years (Reason: FDA recommendations, 10/2008).
- DOSAGE: Determine by finding your child's weight in the top row of the dosage table.
- ADULT DOSAGE: 60 mg maximum.
- FREQUENCY: Repeat every 6 hours as needed.
- AVAILABILITY: Pseudoephedrine products are found behind the counter of pharmacies in response to legislation enacted in 2006. Ask a pharmacist for assistance in obtaining these medications.
- MEASURING THE DOSAGE: Syringes and droppers are more accurate than teaspoons. If possible, use the syringe or dropper that comes with the medication. If you use a teaspoon, it should be a measuring spoon. Regular spoons are not reliable. Also, remember that 1 level teaspoon equals 5 mL and ½ teaspoon equals 2.5 mL.

Index